SpringerBriefs in Social Work

For further volumes:
http://www.springer.com/series/11571

Deborah Western

Gender-based Violence and Depression in Women

A Feminist Group Work Response

 Springer

Deborah Western
Monash University
Caufield East, VIC
Australia

ISSN 2195-3104   ISSN 2195-3112 (electronic)
ISBN 978-1-4614-7531-6   ISBN 978-1-4614-7532-3 (eBook)
DOI 10.1007/978-1-4614-7532-3
Springer New York Heidelberg Dordrecht London

Library of Congress Control Number: 2013937601

Printed on acid-free paper

Springer is part of Springer Science+Business Media (www.springer.com)

Contents

Chapter 1
Introduction

Abstract This chapter provides an introduction to this book with an overview of the central concepts of gender-based violence against women, women's experiences of depression and feminist group work. Introductory coverage of the activity of journaling is provided and initial attention is given to key theoretical and contextual perspectives employed in the understanding and analysis of gender-based violence against women and depression. The feminist group work response through the Women's Journaling Group Program model is introduced.

Keywords Gender-based violence against women · Journaling · Depression · Feminist group work · Critical feminist theory · Women's journaling groups

Gender-based Violence and Depression: Women's Voices

> When I've got a struggle going on, I'll try and write it out. Find out more about myself. (Penny).

Having a sense of meaning and purpose in our lives enables us to engage in the world around us, pursue goals and passions and feel a sense of belonging with family, friends and communities. Women who experience violence and depression commonly lose this sense of meaning and purpose and can struggle to regain, or even develop, this sense. However, the activity of journaling can provide women with a safe space to express their thoughts and feelings, reclaim a sense of identity and meaning, and develop a sense of hope for their future. The creativity inherent in expressing oneself, whether this be through writing, drawing, poetry, collage or other journaling techniques, can encourage and inspire women and, consequently, assist them to understand and to manage their experiences of violence and depression.

Penny's quote, above, shows when and why she journals. Phoebe provides us with insight into the importance and influence of journaling for her:

D. Western, *Gender-based Violence and Depression in Women*,
SpringerBriefs in Social Work, DOI: 10.1007/978-1-4614-7532-3_1,
© The Author(s) 2013

"(My journaling is) about me, my life, joys, pain, suffering and excitement. It entwines and unwinds the complexity of my life. It is self-talk—writing your own narrative. It is multilayered for me, like circles overlapping. It is about me and how I feel about it all; the effects it has on my highs and lows in life".

When women meet in a supportive group to journal together, share experiences, reflect on their learning and plan for changes in their lives, the impact of journaling as a therapeutic activity is strengthened even further. The following journal entries give us an appreciation of the journaling group experience for three women:

> I enjoyed the group discussions and the fact that I did not need to explain or excuse the way I felt about my life.
>
> Provides a useful comparison to the ways others deal with their problems. And the similarity of responses to different situations is very comforting.
>
> It is valuable to listen to others' thoughts, feelings and make these connections to myself. It is good when you realise you are not the only one that feels or thinks some things.

I have begun this book with the voices of women because women's stories can tell us so much about their experiences and yet their voices are often silenced when they are in the midst of violence and depression. Women have informed and participated in the development of the feminist group work response, the Women's Journaling Group Program, which is the feature of this book. Women are also the focus of our attention as we consider possibilities for effective supports, programs and activities that can assist them to understand, manage and begin to recover from their experiences of violence and depression.

This chapter provides an introduction to this book with an overview of the central concepts of gender-based violence against women, women's experiences of depression and feminist group work. Introductory coverage of the activity of journaling is provided and initial attention is given to key theoretical and contextual perspectives employed in the understanding and analysis of gender-based violence against women and depression.

Central Concepts in This Book

The widely recognised definition in the United Nations' Declaration on the Elimination of Violence Against Women states that violence against women is "any act of gender based violence that results in, or is likely to result in, physical, sexual or psychological harm or suffering to women, including threats of such acts, coercion or arbitrary deprivation of liberty, whether occurring in public or private life" (UN 1993). Estimates of the nature and extent of violence against women throughout the world vary and depend on factors such as the countries in which research is undertaken, the methods of data collection and women's preparedness and safety in disclosing or reporting their experiences of violence. Nevertheless, research indicates one in three women experience some form of physical and/or sexual violence in their lifetime.

Gender-based violence against women has short- and long-term impacts for women and these include impacts on women's mental health. A significant impact of gender-based violence for women is depression and this is the focus in this text. Research has established clear links between depression in women and the domestic violence experienced by these women. Beydoun et al. (2012) for example, found a 2–3 times increased risk of major depressive disorder and a 1.5–2 times increased risk of elevated depressive symptoms and postpartum depression among women who had experienced intimate partner violence compared with women who had not experienced this violence. Moreover, women are twice as likely as men to experience depression and approximately 20 % of women are likely to experience depression at some time in their lives.

During my social work practice with women who had experienced sexual assault and family violence, I came to realise that many women journaled about their experiences of violence, particularly their emotional responses, their doubts and fears and the impact the violence had on their lives. Sometimes women jotted down words and brief sentences on whatever they had to hand; other women journaled regularly in notebooks and scrapbooks purchased specifically for the purpose of journaling and reflecting. In counselling sessions, women often mentioned they had journaled about their anger or their depression, for example, and this provided starting points and further prompts for our conversations. Naomi explains the importance of journaling for her:

> I have discovered that journaling is mine, it's something positive for me that I can use to help me see clearly again. It's powerful, more than I was aware. Journaling is about me because it's my writing, it's my thoughts, my feelings and, yeah, I don't have to justify things, I don't have to make it sound wonderful or important or bring in theories or other people's thoughts on it or whatever. It's just raw, sort of thing.

Women have long expressed their thoughts and feelings, recorded their experiences, asked questions and developed a sense of self through the practice of journaling. Journals have provided a safe and private space for women to articulate their concerns and uncertainties and to make sense of what is happening around them. As Naomi suggests in her journal entry, above, journaling can provide a powerful, personal and creative way to learn about oneself and to understand experiences of violence and depression.

My focus on working with women and writing about their experiences of violence, depression and participation in feminist group work has been deliberate. This has resulted from my practice experience in working with women and knowing that women have a higher likelihood of experiencing depression than do men and a higher likelihood of experiencing violence as a result of their gender than do men. From a critical feminist perspective, exploration of the role that gender plays in the development of depression in women and in the perpetration of violence against women in intimate partner relationships is crucial. In addition to the complementary concept of intersectionality, these are the perspectives and the lenses I use in this text to understand, analyse and inform a social work response to both violence against women and the consequent depression experienced by women.

Knowing that many women journal and also knowing about the benefits for women of participating in therapeutic-focused groups with other women, I wondered what might emerge if I combined the activities of journaling and group work in social work practice.

My research with women led to the creation, piloting and final development of a model for a Women's Journaling Group Program. Women's journaling groups are relevant for women who already journal or for women who have not previously journaled but would like to try. The program varies for each group in order to reflect the needs of women in each group. Women are supported to make suggestions about activities and processes. The group sessions are a mixture of facilitated journal activities that focus on women's experiences of depression and violence with opportunities for identification and expression of emotions, thoughts, concerns and questions. As the program moves through the activities, a focus on hope, the future and transformation is introduced. Throughout the sessions women are encouraged to share their ideas and insights that come from their journaling, to witness and support each other and to reflect on their own learnings, development and changes. The group processes and the processes involved in journaling, reflecting and making changes are as important as the outcomes from journaling and discussion activities. Evaluation and reflection questions can be built into the end of sessions so that the women can spend time to think about their experiences and to provide feedback to facilitators about how they are experiencing the group. Women are, therefore, involved as participants but also have a role as group reviewers and developers. This reflects a strong feminist value of participation.

Groups can be structured to run over the course of one or two days or over weekly sessions. The overall aim is for women to have a clearer and deeper understanding of themselves, the impacts of depression and violence, the contributing factors to violence against women and subsequent depression, a stronger sense of self and self-confidence and the development of new skills.

The model is premised on gendered and critical feminist understandings of violence against women, depression in women and the facilitation of groups for women. Feminist counselling principles and methods of consciousness-raising and resistance underpin the activities and the focus of the journaling group model. These activities also open possibilities for women to make connections between their own experiences of violence and depression, the experiences of other women and the attitudinal, structural and systemic factors that perpetuate the continuation of violence against women.

I believe that a critical feminist understanding of violence against women and women's subsequent experiences of depression is vital because it enables us to take a broad contextual view of the contributors to and dynamics of this violence and depression. This removes the focus on each individual woman as somehow responsible for feeling depressed or experiencing violence. Clearly, responsibility for gender-based violence against women belongs with the perpetrator of the violence. Indeed, as we consider the ways in which we may reduce and prevent violence against women, we see that everyone within all communities has a role to play.

Throughout this text, I include comments from women who contributed to the development of the Women's Journaling Group Program and from women who have participated in the Program. Their comments help to bring alive the text and invite us into some personal and insightful thoughts about the ways in which journaling assisted them to understand, manage and begin to recover from their depression.

Women employ a variety of journaling techniques and these demonstrate that women's journaling involves much more than the traditional form of prose writing. This is exciting because it opens up the potential of journaling as a therapeutic social work method. For women who do not like writing or do not have writing skills, journaling can include drawing, painting, reflecting and performing. Journaling is a flexible and creative process and the ways in which women journal—and express themselves—may be as therapeutic as the end result.

Women's Journaling Groups are of most benefit to women with mild to moderate depression and who are well enough to attend a group regularly. I am mindful that this will not be possible for many women and this also reminds us to think about how women in different situations and circumstances throughout the world might experience violence and its consequences. Whilst journaling may not be possible or appealing for all women, the principles of consciousness-raising and resistance which underpin the Women's Journaling Group Program model may provide a framework for women to respond to violence and depression in other ways. For example, in a revision of the traditional activity of sharing experiences and narratives, Sowards and Renegar (2006) suggested that sharing stories could be seen as a form of feminist activism and thus, consciousness-raising, resistance and action even if it occurs on an individual basis. I explore these principles and methods of consciousness-raising and resistance in more detail in Chap. 6.

The aim of this book is to provide practitioners with theoretical, conceptual and practice-based information and ideas to guide them in their work with women who have experienced violence and depression. The practice response within the book is based on feminist group work and specifically focuses on a model for Women's Journaling Groups. The theoretical and conceptual information and ideas provide solid foundations for informed, considered and reflective social work practice with women who have experienced violence and depression. In introducing a model for Women's Journaling Groups, I do so in such a way that practitioners may use the research-based ideas and knowledge to facilitate women's journaling groups themselves. I hope that the theoretical and conceptual information provided will encourage practitioners to structure women's journaling groups in ways that acknowledge, respond to and reflect the unique needs of each woman in each group, yet also provide women with a sense of shared experience and belonging in their group.

The book is written in such a way that readers can read the book from start to finish or can dip into chapters that are of particular interest to them. I begin by providing a conceptual and contextual background for theorising and under-standing gender-based violence and depression in women. I then introduce the terms 'gender-based violence' and 'violence against women' and look at some global data and a human rights framework to provide a background and context on which to base our knowledge of the problem. I then move onto looking at women's experiences of depression, what is specific to the ways in which depression fre-quently develops for women and the links between violence against women and depression. I also include some theoretical information that assists us to under-stand depression in women as well as an overview of concepts that are integral to the consideration of recovery.

Next, consideration of concepts important to group facilitation, including feminist group work theory and practice, and the methods of consciousness-raising and resistance is given. In a more practice-oriented section of the book, I spend some time exploring the practice of journaling and journal therapy; that is, the use of writing for therapeutic purposes. Following this, I introduce the model of the Women's Journaling Group Program. Within this chapter, we see that journaling is a process and a form of action rather than a passive, isolated pastime which women undertake. The model consists of two overarching frameworks, one which forms quite a reflective component of journaling and the other which establishes an active and dynamic component. In addition, four major narratives and various threads provide guidelines and inspiration for the development of journaling activities within Women's Journaling Groups. Finally, I include some practice guidelines for those readers who are interested in developing and facilitating their own versions of a Women's Journaling Group.

The Women Researchers and Participants in This Book

I would like to introduce to you the women who contributed to the development of the model for the Women's Journaling Group Program and whose comments appear throughout the text. They are: Jessica, Naomi, Adair, Deb, Susan, Phoebe, Barbra, Samantha, Penny, Zelda, Adella, Vivienne, Rachael, Zoe, Magdalena and Kate.

The women came from regional areas in the state of Victoria in Australia and from Melbourne, the capital city of Victoria. They ranged in age from early twenties to their sixties. Some were married, one or two divorced or separated, some never married. Most women had children, some had grandchildren, and all had contact with children such as nephews and nieces in their families. Some women worked, some had retired and some were having a break. Women worked as artists, business owners, students and in the health and welfare fields. Some of the women had been formally diagnosed with depression, most had self-diagnosed and all had received some health or medical support, particularly from their general practitioner. Some women had been very unwell in the past; all were well now although not necessarily feeling one hundred per cent. One of the criteria for attending the groups was that they were well enough to attend all the sessions, barring unanticipated disruptions.

So a huge big thank you to all these women. They will guide you through this text as their ideas, journaling, feedback and discussions illustrate the ways in which Women's Journaling Groups can be facilitated, the types of narratives and themes that are important to consider in journaling activities and the different meanings and understandings that can be made of women's experiences of violence and depression.

Chapter 2 provides us with a brief glimpse into a session of a Women's Journaling Group where we can gain a sense of how such a group might be facilitated and how journaling activities can be employed to explore women's experiences of violence and depression.

References

Beydoun H, Beydoun M, Kaufman J, Lo B, Zonderman A (2012) Intimate partner violence against adult women and its association with major depressive disorder, depressive symptoms and post-partum depression: a systematic review and meta-analysis. Soc Sci Med 75(6):959–975

Sowards S, Renegar V (2006) Reconceptualising rhetorical activism in contemporary feminist contexts. Howard J Commun 17:57–74

United Nations (1993) Declaration on the elimination of violence against women. http://www.un-documents.net/a48r104.htm. Accessed 1 Jan 2013

Chapter 2
An Introductory Visit to a Women's Journaling Group

Abstract This chapter provides a brief glimpse into a session of a Women's Journaling Group where readers can gain a sense of how such a group might be facilitated and how journaling activities can be employed to explore women's experiences of violence and depression.

Keywords Journaling · Women · Gender-based violence · Depression · Women's journaling groups

A Women's Journaling Group

In this chapter I would like to invite you to observe part of a group session with the women as they participate in a Women's Journaling Group Program.

Facilitator: "Good evening everyone. How are you?"

The women reply in different voices and with different responses.

"I'm good!"
"I'm hungry; can we eat as we talk?"
"It's freezing outside. What happened to the summer weather?"
"Sorry I'm late, the dog escaped".

Following some laughs and shared snippets of conversation, the women find their seats around a table that holds pens, paper, magazines, glue, scissors, books, other journaling paraphernalia, women's baskets and purses and food for a light supper.

As facilitator I ask them how their week has been and what journaling they might have practised since we last met. Some women have been busy and not able to journal their thoughts or feelings, but other women share their experiences. There is a mixture of excitement at new insights into the impacts of verbal violence, doubt about uncovered responses from the past and pride at taking steps towards a new goal of beginning friendships with other mothers at the children's school. As the women listen to each other, they encourage each other and comment on the changes that have occurred. There is some gentle challenging when one woman wonders if all her efforts to re-establish a new lifestyle are worth it. The other women remind her she has rights to live free from violence and that depression is a common response for women who have experienced violence. The atmosphere is friendly, reassuring, trusting and safe.

In response to my suggestion we start some journaling, the women agree and organise their journaling materials. I will use a journaling technique the women have used before but will provide a different topic and context. The technique is a 'sentence starter' and I read it out to the women. Their journaling activity is to complete the gaps in the sentence with whatever comes into their minds.

Me: "It is important to me for my voice and my needs to be heard because ... and then my depression ...".

When women have finished their journaling and have thought and shared quietly with each other, we do a round where each woman can share whatever she would like to share about her response. Some women read out exactly what they journaled. Other women talk generally about what they journaled and the themes that arose. Some women add insights that were revealed.

Adella wondered why it was important to be heard. "Why do we need other people to validate us and our thoughts?"

Zoe journaled that "It is important for me to voice my needs and have them heard when I'm depressed because often I feel that's when they're totally taken away. When I'm depressed, I'm so lost within myself, that when I do express myself, I'm taking a huge risk of putting myself out there. And often my thoughts might be jumbled and quite inarticulate. If I do that, often the depression can ease, if only for a minute or so, if someone actually hears me, the power of that. When you're struggling so hard to express your needs. Even if they don't understand it, they've actually taken the time".

Penny journaled "Because if I'm not heard, I lose sight of who I am, what I think, or I lose touch with my feelings. It makes it more difficult to express them and then I feel out of control and not in touch with myself. Gets too difficult to express myself, so I go into myself and other people's needs are more important".

Zelda journaled "Because the hearing validates me. Not just others hearing me, but me hearing me. I also need to be heard while I'm speaking without shouting. If I get into shouting mode, I'm already uncertain that my opinion is valid or my needs are reasonable. And then my depression rolls in again, like a fog, surrounding me to the extent that I cannot see my way, so I go and hide away. To write this down, feels like a new learning".

Magdalena said: "Because they need to be recognised".

We finished this activity with some further discussion and each woman highlighted what was most enlightening for her. This journaling activity opens up further opportunities for women to keep journaling and to think about, for example, what are the 'needs' that are important for them to identify and achieve. As one woman later journaled in a 6-week evaluation follow-up: "Depression that I've experienced I think has partly (or mostly) been about my issues with not knowing myself and so not knowing my priorities & needs, so exploring this has given me insight to my depression/causes of my depression".

Conclusion

This excerpt has provided a brief glimpse into one particular session of a women's journaling group. It shows how women may interact and support each other, how insights might be achieved through journaling, reflection and discussion within the group and, outside the group in between sessions, and how a focus on expressing thoughts and feelings can be combined with a focus on hope and moving toward change. In the following chapters I look at the theories, concepts, contexts and perspectives that are helpful in gaining an understanding of and ability to analyse gender-based violence against women and depression in women. I will also explore how this knowledge underpins and supports the Women's Journaling Group Program model.

Chapter 3
A Conceptual and Contextual Background for Gender-based Violence and Depression in Women

Abstract This chapter provides an overview of the central concepts in this text before a more in-depth exploration in later chapters. The central concepts are gender-based violence against women; the notion of gender; depression in women; human rights and public health frameworks; critical feminist theories; the concept of intersectionality and its contribution to critical feminist theoretical understandings and the links between violence against women and the subsequent development of depression in women. This overview also provides a context within which an understanding of the central concepts and of the rationale and underpinnings of the Women's Journaling Group Programme model can be situated.

Keywords Gender · Violence against women · Gender-based violence · Critical feminist theory · Intersectionality · Public health · Human rights · Prevalence

Conceptual and Contextual Background: Gender-based Violence Against Women

In November 2012, the United Nations emphasised the urgent responsibility that countries have to implement national policies to end gender-based violence against women, calling such violence, one of the most pervasive human rights violations worldwide. At an event to mark the annual International Day for the Elimination of Violence Against Women, UN Secretary-General Ban Ki-Moon reminded the world that "Each and every State has an obligation to develop or improve the relevant laws, policies and plans, bring perpetrators to justice and provide remedies to women who have been subjected to violence" (UN News Centre 2012).

Violence against women is an endemic problem throughout the world. Women are subject to violence in refugee camps, in evacuation areas, in regions devastated by natural disasters and violence that is used as a weapon of war and power in

D. Western, *Gender-based Violence and Depression in Women*,
SpringerBriefs in Social Work, DOI: 10.1007/978-1-4614-7532-3_3,
© The Author(s) 2013

conflict and post-conflict zones. But women also experience violence in non-conflict areas and as True (2012, p. 5) notes, "… it is the gendered social and economic inequalities between women and men that make women most vulnerable to violence and abuse in whatever context". Moreover, innumerable women are subject to violence within their homes and communities, commonly from someone known to them, most often a current or previous male partner within an intimate relationship. In writing about the parallels in the trauma experienced by soldiers and victims in war and women in domestic violence, Herman wrote evocatively of the commonalities '… between the survivors of vast concentration camps created by tyrants who rule nations and the survivors of small, hidden concentration camps created by tyrants who rule their homes' (Herman 1992, p. 3).

In establishing the context for the way in which the concept of gender-based violence against women is understood and employed in this book, an important consideration is the use of terminology. Different terms referring to gender-based violence are employed in different countries and regions throughout the world. For example in Victoria, Australia, the term 'family violence' rather than 'domestic violence' is increasingly used in discussion, debate, policy and legislation. This has largely resulted from the recognition of the many different forms of violence that may occur within families and the wide preference from Aboriginal communities for 'family violence' which reflects the extensive understanding of family that many indigenous communities have. The Victorian Indigenous Family Violence Taskforce (2003, p. 123) defined family violence as: 'An issue focused around a wide range of physical, emotional, sexual, social, spiritual, cultural, psychological and economic abuses that occur within families, intimate relationships, extended families, kinship networks and communities. It extends to one-on-one fighting, abuse of Indigenous community workers, as well as self-harm, injury and suicide'.

Myriad other terms are employed throughout the world, perhaps the best known of which include 'intimate partner violence', 'domestic violence', 'domestic abuse' and 'violence against women'. In this text, I use the terms 'gender-based violence against women' and 'violence against women' to refer to the violence experienced by women from male perpetrators (most often known to them) and to enable an analysis and understanding of this violence from a strong gender-based perspective. The term 'gender-based violence' can also be used to refer to violence experienced by men as a result of their gender and so does not specifically refer solely to violence experienced by women. However, it is a term that is used broadly throughout the world and the use of the word 'gender' initiates thinking about the differences in the ways that women and men experience, and are subject to, violence particularly from someone known to them. The term 'violence against women' clearly and unambiguously states the nature of the violence and the problem to be addressed.

Prevalence and Impacts of Gender-based Violence Against Women

Notwithstanding the complexities of undertaking research and collecting data around gender-based violence, a picture of the extent of global violence against women does emerge. Research has consistently documented that violence against women is a gendered occurrence and a gendered crime (Garcia-Moreno and Watts 2011; UN 1993; Reed et al. 2010) and it is estimated that one in three women throughout the world will experience physical and/or sexual violence at some point in their lives. A multi-country study, mainly in developing nations, found that between 15 and 71 % of women aged 15–49 years reported physical and/or sexual violence by an intimate partner at some point in their lives (World Health Organisation 2005). International data compiled by UN Women (2010) suggested that between 15 and 76 % of women are likely to experience physical and/or sexual violence in their lifetime. In the Australian component of the International Violence Against Women Survey, over a third of women reported experiencing physical and/or sexual violence since the age of 16 (Mouzos and Makkai 2004).

Physical, sexual, psychological and economic gender-based violence against women have short- and long-term impacts for women which include physical injury and illness, mental ill-health, post-traumatic stress, drug and alcohol use, poverty and homicide/femicide. Children exposed to this violence frequently experience fear, insecurity, trauma and may be injured or killed themselves (Kirkwood 2012). Other implications, although perhaps less obvious but still of significant concern, include women's inability to find and maintain employment, loss of accommodation, children's, sometimes frequent, relocation from their schools and childcare settings and the health, legal, justice and economic costs to the community. I look further at the impacts and implications of violence against women in Chap. 4.

Conceptual and Contextual Background: Why is Gender Important?

Gender plays a role in the occurrence of gender-based violence against women and in the depression experienced by women. Gender refers to more than simply the biological sex differences between males and females, but to the broad differences that exist between men and women in their day-to-day life experiences. Alston (2013, p. 96) writes that "Gender refers to the different ways women and men operate within socially constructed, sanctioned roles that subsequently shape the ways individuals respond to circumstances and events". Gender and its consequences also shape communities, cultures, and countries and is a learned way of being.

Gender differentially impacts men's and women's access to, ownership of and influence over power and resources, employment, land ownership, income, safe and secure accommodation, political representation and other roles in society. Violence against women is significantly enabled by gender inequality, and conversely gender-based violence is seen as a major contributor to gender inequality. Moreover, gender is closely linked to attitudes to women and to violence against women. Meyering (2011) concludes that attitudes to gender equality are the key predictor of attitudes to domestic violence. So people who do not hold gender equality as a key value or aim within their community tend to understand domestic violence as largely insignificant, uncommon and equally perpetrated by men and women. I further explore contributing factors to violence against women in the Chap. 4.

Gender is also an important consideration for practitioners when working with women experiencing depression. Astbury (2001, p. 2) notes that gender is "a structural determinant of mental health and mental illness" and, due to the high numbers of women experiencing depression throughout the world, urges that causes of this depression be identified and eradicated. She believes "This requires a multi-level, intersectoral approach, gendered mental health policy with a public health focus and gender-specific risk factor reduction strategies, as well as gender sensitive services and equitable access to them" (Astbury 2001, p. 2). Later in this chapter, I look at the roles that public health frameworks and integrated and gendered approaches to the response to and prevention of violence against women can take.

Conceptual and Contextual Background: Human Rights and Public Health Frameworks

As knowledge of the nature, extent and impact of violence against women has expanded in the last few decades, new perspectives have been employed in order to understand and provide contexts and frameworks for responding to this violence. Violence against women is now acknowledged as a violation of women's human rights. The use of a human rights perspective and framework to understand and analyse the dynamics of violence against women and to consider how best to respond, reduce and eliminate it, reframes the violence from a largely insignificant, inconsequential, hidden occurrence to a visible, highly dangerous and prevalent global problem for which all individuals and communities have responsibility. A human rights framework reminds us that gender-based violence against women is a form of discrimination and prohibits women from enjoying rights such as liberty and security of the person; freedom from wrongful gender stereotyping and freedom from torture or cruel, inhuman or degrading treatment or punishment (Cusack 2009).

Building on the human rights framework is an emerging understanding of gender-based violence as a public health issue (Beydoun et al. 2012; Garcia-Moreno and Watts 2011; Nakray 2013; Western and Mason 2013). This has largely resulted from the increased global awareness of the nature and extent of violence against women, the efforts to cost the impacts of this violence, the growing community attention given to increasingly personalised accounts of this violence and calls for action to respond to and to eliminate gender-based violence against women. A public health approach includes a strong emphasis on primary prevention. Primary prevention strategies in relation to violence against women aim to prevent violence from occurring and include, for example educational activities exploring and strengthening beliefs and attitudes towards gender equality. Secondary prevention, or early intervention (VicHealth 2007), refers to activities and services that are provided in response to early signs of violence in efforts to prevent the violence from escalating and becoming entrenched and enabling those at risk to access safety strategies and plans. Tertiary prevention, or intervention (VicHealth 2007), is provided after violence has occurred and includes support, advocacy, crisis and counselling services for women and their children, behaviour change programmes for perpetrators and criminal and civil justice responses such as intervention orders.

Governments and communities are seeking and providing increased funding and focus on primary prevention in relation to violence against women. This marks significant progression and development in recognising the huge damage that occurs from violence against women throughout the world. However, funding, policy and programmatic development and legislative and other reforms cannot ignore tertiary prevention activities while violence still occurs. The focus of this book is providing a therapeutic, motivating and galvanising response for women who had experienced violence and depression. One such response is the provision of feminist group work. An initial consideration of a feminist group work response clearly locates such an activity within tertiary prevention strategies. However, the activities within group work and the dynamics and relationships that develop amongst group members during group work frequently result in members learning new skills, developing confidence in themselves to take action and to link with new friends and previously unaccessed services. These achievements can shift therapeutic group work into the arena of secondary prevention and, possibly, primary prevention.

This example of situating a feminist group work response in a public health framework highlights the difficulties and disadvantages of separating the different levels of prevention and the strategies within each level. As social workers, we work well when we work across and within different levels, systems, services and strategies. One of the strengths of the recent Family Violence Reform Strategy in the family violence sector in Victoria, Australia is the emphasis on the importance of creating and working within a 'joined-up' service system and multi-sectoral service delivery approach (Ross et al. 2011; Western and Mason 2013). An effective coordinated and collaborative structure has a good chance of meeting the varied and complex needs of women and their children who experience violence and the needs of men who use violence against women. In such a structure, the links between primary, secondary and tertiary prevention strategies and activities can be identified and strengthened. So when facilitating feminist group work through the Women's Journaling Group Programme model, our practice is strengthened when we integrate it with other supports, resources and programmes in which women are involved.

Conceptual and Contextual Background: Critical Feminist Theoretical Understandings and Intersectionality

Whilst this text is primarily practice focused, it is crucial to be clear about the theoretical underpinnings to practice, given the recursive relationship between theory and practice where each continuously informs and builds on the other. In addition to working within the human rights framework and to ensure a strong gender lens and analysis is employed in the response to violence against women, I employ a critical feminist theoretical understanding when analysing and examining this violence. A critical feminist understanding of violence against women, and of depression experienced by women, enables me to watch for, monitor and integrate into practice an awareness of structural and systemic inequalities and power distributions. It also reminds me to look for, to hear and to acknowledge women's perspectives, narratives and understandings of their experiences with violence, depression and recovery and incorporate these into my knowledge and practice. A critical feminist perspective holds that the personal is political, that diversity amongst women must be recognised, that transformation and change provide foci for social work with women and that responsibility for understanding and preventing the development and experience of violence and depression in women must be a multifactorial, multi-level societal commitment.

Further, a critical feminist theorising of gender-based violence against women provides scope to add to practice and analysis the concept and guiding principles of intersectionality; a concept that enables a more thorough exploration of structural and systemic contributors to violence against women and their depression by looking not only at gender, but at additional and intersecting forms of oppression such as race, ethnicity, class and sexuality (Sokoloff and Dupont 2005). Debates about the ways in which intersectionality may be defined and/or conceptualised impede a simple explanation. Davis (2008, p. 67) provides a loose description of intersectionality as "the interaction of multiple identities and experiences of exclusion and subordination".

In thinking about women's experiences of, not only gender-based violence, but the depression that many women subsequently experience, an intersectional, critical and feminist understanding enables me to consider the contributions, impacts and consequences that intersecting factors of gender, race, ethnicity, age, (dis)ability, class and sexuality may have on different women's experiences of inequality, oppression and marginalisation. Such an understanding and analysis also enables us to see the varied barriers and difficulties imposed on women attempting to recover from depression and become safe from violence. I do this in an effort to make visible and recognise the experiences of violence against women from varying backgrounds, locations and positions and, following Nixon and Humphreys (2010), to contribute to the continuing development of feminist theorising around violence against women. Nixon and Humphreys (2010, p. 139) note the importance of "creating a more nuanced and sophisticated understanding of (violence against women) and how it can differentially affect those who experience and survive abuse".

Conceptual and Contextual Background: Links Between Violence Against Women and Impacts on Women's Mental Health

As noted earlier, violence against women has short- and long-term impacts for women and these include impacts on women's mental health. Research has established clear links between depression in women and domestic violence experienced by women (Filson et al. 2010; Vos et al. 2006). The Access Economics research undertaken in Australia in (2004) found that almost 18 % of all depression in women in Australia was associated with domestic violence. The Australian National Survey of Mental Health and Wellbeing (2007) found that over a quarter of the surveyed women had experienced some form of gender-based violence and that this violence was also linked to mental illnesses including depression, anxiety and suicide attempts. In a metaanalysis of observational studies in the research literature between 1980 and 2010—mostly from Western countries—Beydoun et al. (2012) found a 2–3 times increased risk of major depressive disorder and a 1.5–2 times increased risk of elevated depressive symptoms and postpartum depression among women who had experienced intimate partner violence compared with women who had not experienced this violence. These authors also estimated that between 9 and 28 % of the depression (major depressive disorder, elevated depressive symptoms and post-natal depression) experienced by women was attributable to experiencing domestic violence over their lifetime. Emerging research shows connections between intimate partner violence and the existence of depressive symptoms in women (even when adjusted for other possible contributing factors such as previous depression) in the first 12 months after childbirth.

In an analysis of data from the World Health Organisation's multi-country study on women's health and domestic violence against women, Devries et al. (2011) found that the prevalence of suicide attempts in women ranged from 0.8 (Tanzania) to 12 % (Peru), although suicidal thoughts throughout a woman's lifetime occurred in as many as 29 % of the women. These researchers found that intimate partner violence was the highest risk factor (after taking into account possible mental illness) for suicide attempts. The links between depression and suicide/suicide attempts are well-known.

Some researchers have also explored the consequences of depression itself on women's perceptions of the violence directed against them, their rights to live without violence and their abilities to recover from the depression. Calvete et al. (2007) found that women, particularly those who had experienced psychological violence, often felt unable to influence or cope with their situation, held little hope that their situation could change and were uncertain about being able to rely on individuals or services for support or assistance. In addition, women felt there was something inherently wrong with them because of the violence they experienced and because of the difficulties they felt they had in coping with the violence. These perceptions, in turn, could lead to deeper depression for women as they 'disengaged' from attempts to seek support in understanding the impact of the violence on them. Similarly, Filson et al. (2010) further validated knowledge that women who experience domestic violence frequently feel powerlessness in the relationship and in their ability to change their situation. Violence used by men includes significant degrees of power and control. Filson et al. (2010) conclude that intimate partner violence can affect depression in women through creating a sense of powerlessness. Traditional and rigid gender roles that are often enforced by men who use violence also take away power and control from women because of the expectation that women will be passive and dependent, be responsible for the care of others and for unpaid domestic and agricultural labour.

Conclusion

These are important findings to consider when looking at the three levels of violence prevention in the public health framework and the strategies and activities within each level. In relation to a feminist support group for women experiencing depression as a result of gender-based violence, the consideration of the issue of powerlessness in women is paramount. I will explore this notion further in Chap. 8 when I introduce the model of the Women's Journaling Group Programme. In the Chap. 4, I look in some more detail at key concepts in this text.

References

Access Economics (2004) The cost of domestic violence to the Australian economy: parts 1 & 2. Partnerships against domestic violence. Commonwealth of Australia, Canberra

Alston M (2013) Gender-based violence in post-disaster recovery situations: an emerging public health issue. In: Keerty Nakray (ed) Gender-based violence and public health. Routledge, London and New York, pp 95–107

Astbury J (2001) Gender disparities in mental health. In: Mental health: ministerial round tables 2001, 54th world health assemble. World Health Organisation, Geneva

Australian Bureau of Statistics (2007) National survey of mental health and wellbeing: summary of results. Australian Bureau of Statistics, Canberra

Beydoun H, Beydoun M, Kaufman J, Lo B, Zonderman A (2012) Intimate partner violence against adult women and its association with major depressive disorder, depressive symptoms and post-partum depression: a systematic review and meta-analysis. Soc Sci Med 75(6):959–975

Calvete E, Corral S, Estévez A (2007) Cognitive and coping mechanisms in the interplay between intimate partner violence and depression. Anxiety Stress Coping Int J 20(4):369–382

Cusack S (2009) Advancing women's rights through human rights law: possibilities and practical action. University of New South Wales. Australian Domestic and Family Violence Clearinghouse, Sydney

Davis K (2008) Intersectionality as buzzword: a sociology of science perspective on what makes a feminist theory successful. Feminist Theor 9(1):67–85

Department of Victorian Communities (2003) The indigenous family violence task force—final report, 123. Department of Victorian Communities, Victoria

Devries K, Watts C, Yoshihama M, Kiss L, Schraiber L, Deyessa N, Heise L, Durand J, Mbwambo J, Jansen H, Berhane Y, Ellsberg M, Garcia-Moreno C (2011) Violence against women is strongly associated with suicide attempts: evidence from the WHO multi-country study on women's health and domestic violence against women. Soc Sci Med 73:79–86

Filson J, Ulloa E, Runfola C, Hokoda A (2010) Does powerlessness explain the relationship between intimate partner violence and depression? J Interpers Violence 25(3):400–415

Garcia-Moreno C, Watts C (2011) Violence against women: an urgent public health priority. Bull World Health Organ 89(2):2–3

Herman J (1992) Trauma and recovery: from domestic abuse to political terror. Basic Books, London

Kirkwood D (2012) 'Just say goodbye'. Parents who kill their children in the context of separation. Discussion Paper No. 8. Domestic Violence Resource Centre Victoria, Melbourne

Meyering I (2011) What factors shape community attitudes to domestic violence? University of New South Wales. Australian Domestic and Family Violence Clearinghouse, Sydney

Mouzos J, Makkai T (2004) Women's experiences of male violence: findings from the Australian component of the international violence against women survey (IVAWS). Canberra: Australian Institute of Criminology, Research and Public Policy Series, No. 56

Nakray K (2013) Gender-based violence: a framework for public health budgets and policies. In: Nakray K (ed) Gender-based violence and public health. Routledge, London, pp 15–29

Nixon J, Humphreys C (2010) Marshalling the evidence: using intersectionality in the domestic violence frame. Soc Polit 17(2):137–158

Reed E, Raj A, Miller E, Silverman J (2010) Losing the "Gender" in gender-based violence: the missteps of research on dating and intimate partner violence. Violence Against Women 16(3):348–354

Ross S, Frere M, Healey L, Humphreys C (2011) A whole of government strategy for family violence reform. Aust J Public Adm 70(2):131–142

Sokoloff N, Dupont I (2005) Domestic violence at the intersections of race, class and gender: challenges and contributions to understanding violence against marginalized women in diverse communities. Violence Against Women 11(1):38–64

True J (2012) The political economy of violence against women. Oxford University Press, New York

UN News Centre (2012) States have obligation to eliminate violence against women—UN officials. http://www.un.org/apps/news/story.asp?NewsID=43624 Accessed 7 Jan 2013

UN Women (2010) Virtual Knowledge Centre to end violence against women and girls. http://www.endvawnow.org/en/articles/299-fast-facts-statistics-on-violence-against-women-and-girls-.html Accessed 28 May 2013

United Nations (1993) UN Declaration on the Elimination of Violence against Women. Geneva

VicHealth (2007) Preventing violence before it occurs: a framework and background paper to guide the primary prevention of violence against women in Victoria. Melbourne: Victorian Health Promotion Foundation.

Vos T, Astbury J, Piers L, Magnus A, Heenan M, Stanley L, Walker L, Webster K (2006) Measuring the impact of intimate partner violence on the health of women in Victoria, Australia. Bull World Health Organ 84:739–744

Western D, Mason R (2013) Gender-based violence in Australia: a state-based joined-up approach. In: Nakray Keerty (ed) Gender-based violence and public health. Routledge, London, pp 79–92

World Health Organisation (2005) WHO multi-country study on women's health and domestic violence against women: summary report of initial results on prevalence, health outcomes and women's responses. Geneva, World Health Organization

Chapter 4
Gender-based Violence Against Women and Human Rights

Abstract This chapter builds on the previous chapters by looking into more depth at some of the central concepts employed in this text. Gender-based violence against women is contextualised in more detail by reviewing key global definitions and estimations of the worldwide nature and frequency of this violence. Contributing factors to the occurrence and continuation of gender-based violence are presented within human rights and public health perspectives as introduced in Chap. 3. Ideas around the prevention and response to gender-based violence begin to take shape. A feminist group work response fits most obviously within a response intervention. However, with the focus of consciousness raising and resistance in the Women's Journalling Group Programme, this group work response also contains elements of prevention and transformation within it.

Keywords Gender-based violence · Human rights · Violence against women · Definitions · Prevalence · Ecological model · Impacts of violence against women · Gender equality · Stereotypes · Beliefs

Global attention to the scale, nature and impact of violence against women, has increased in the last few decades. Following the adoption of the Convention on the Elimination of all forms of Discrimination Against Women (CEDAW) in 1979, the Declaration on the Elimination of Violence Against Women in 1993 by the United Nations General Assembly, and the addition of the Beijing Platform for Action in (1995), gender-based violence against women has slowly, yet progressively, been recognised as a violation of women's basic human rights. In response, various efforts have been made to respond to reduce and eliminate this violence. This has occurred through strengthening and maintaining women's safety and their involvement in social, political and economic activities, introducing legislative and policy reform, encouraging attitudinal change, placing responsibility for violence on perpetrators and emboldening communities to be active in preventing this violence.

The goal of the CEDAW is to eliminate gender discrimination, although it does not refer specifically to the issue of violence against women. Women's human rights and equality are highlighted in the emphasis on ensuring equal access to the benefits of family, employment, the law, education and health care services. Attention is also given to traditional roles and stereotypes of men and women as well as social and cultural practices in society that give rise to discrimination against women. The Declaration on the Elimination of Violence Against Women defines what constitutes violence against women and calls for countries and organisations to take action to prevent and eliminate it. The Beijing Platform for Action also emphasises gender equality and the importance of removing barriers to women's participation in public and private sectors. Regarding the contributing factors to violence against women, the following points are of interest:

- The use of violence against women as a weapon of war and in conflict situations (Point 11)
- The feminisation of poverty and unemployment (Point 17)
- The use of religious extremism to carry out violence or discrimination against women (Point 24)
- Women's under-representation in leadership of political and administrative organisations (Point 28)
- Increased barriers for Indigenous women (Point 32)
- Discrimination against women (Point 38)
- Discrimination and violence against girls, including female infanticide, prenatal sex selection and child marriage (Point 39).

Despite the progress, violence against women remains a critical concern throughout the world. Prior to examining some data and information about the existence and prevalence of violence against women, defining what is meant by violence against women is important. This will then also provide a context in which the concept of gender-based violence against women is employed in this book.

Definitions and Behaviours that Constitute Gender-based Violence Against Women

The widely recognised definition in the United Nations' Declaration on the Elimination of Violence Against Women states that violence against women is "any act of gender based violence that results in, or is likely to result in, physical, sexual or psychological harm or suffering to women, including threats of such acts, coercion or arbitrary deprivation of liberty, whether occurring in public or private life" (UN 1993).

Article 2 of the Declaration outlines the behaviours that constitute violence against women. They include physical, sexual and psychological violence that occurs within the family, the general community and/or violence that is perpetrated or condoned by the State. Violence includes physical assault, marital rape, sexual abuse of female children in the household, dowry-related violence, female genital mutilation and other traditional practices harmful to women, non-spousal violence, violence related to exploitation including trafficking and forced prostitution, and sexual harassment and intimidation at work, in educational institutions and elsewhere.

Countries and states throughout the world have varying definitions and legislation relevant to violence against women. Globally, legislation varies in the breadth of coverage of acts that constitute violence and also varies in the extent to which it is enforced and enforceable.

In a progressive review and redevelopment of legislation in the state of Victoria, Australia in (2008), the new Family Violence Protection Act recognises family violence as behaviour that is threatening, coercive or physically, sexually, emotionally, psychologically and/or economically abusive. Behaviour that controls or dominates a family member and causes that person to feel fear for the safety or wellbeing of their family is also considered to constitute family violence. Examples of the different behaviours are provided; economic abuse includes being prevented from attaining employment, accessing joint financial assets or being coerced to claim social security payments. Emotional or psychological abuse includes name calling and racial taunts, threats to commit suicide and preventing a family member from seeing other family members and friends.

Protection for children is also provided in the legislation because family violence is considered to have occurred if children overhear or witness any of the abusive behaviours stated in the Act. The definition of people who constitute a family member is quite broad and, importantly, includes carers of people with a disability.

The Incidence and Impacts of Gender-based Violence Against Women

Estimating the incidence of violence against women is problematic for various reasons including the secrecy that surrounds violence; reluctance by women to report and disclose violence; varying definitions of what constitutes violence against women; limited financial, measurement and evaluative resources and difficulties in accessing the existing or collaborative data. However, global statistics estimate that a third of the world's women have experienced violence from someone they know, often their partner or another family member. Results from research undertaken in 10 countries by the World Health Organisation (WHO) (2005, p. 5) indicated that the proportion of ever-partnered women who had ever experienced physical or sexual violence, or both, by an intimate partner ranged from 15 to 71 %. Between 13 and 61 % of women had experienced physical violence from a male partner. The proportion of women who had experienced sexual violence ranged from 6 to 59 % of women. Intimate partner sexual violence commonly involves repeated and severe physical and sexual assault with extreme risks to women's safety (Duncan and Western 2011). Underscoring the concern with this violence against women is a number of research findings. For example, more than 25 % of women in the WHO survey (other than in Japan) had been physically or sexually assaulted at least once since the age of 15 with rates as high as 50 % for some countries. In the Australian component of the International Violence Against Women Survey, over a third of women reported experiencing physical and/or sexual violence since the age of 16 (Mouzos and Makkai 2004).

Even scarcer research complicates the estimation of the prevalence of gender-based violence for women who are generally considered to be at higher risk of violence. Indigenous women throughout the world are thought to be up to 40 times more likely to be victims of family violence (B.C. Government 2005; Cripps and Davis 2012; Department of Planning and Community Development 2008; National Clearinghouse on Family Violence 2008). Women with disabilities are at much greater risk of gender-based violence than women without disabilities (Healey et al. 2008), and immigrant women also frequently face higher risks with violence taking additional forms such as exclusion from family and communities and threats of deportation (Ammar et al. 2012; Anitha 2011; Lacey et al. 2013). Women are known to be at higher risk of violence during and after pregnancy. For example, The Personal Safety Survey undertaken in Australia in 2005 found that 59 % of women who had experienced violence by a previous partner since the age of 15 were pregnant at some time during the relationship. Of these women, 36 % reported that violence had occurred when they were pregnant and 17 % that violence occurred for the first time when they were pregnant.

The consequences and impacts of violence against women vary and include physical injuries such as broken bones, cuts and burns, chronic pain, post-traumatic stress, mental illness including depression and anxiety, unwanted pregnancy, sexually transmitted infections including HIV and reproductive health problems, miscarriage and pre-term delivery, suicide, drug and/or alcohol (mis)use, trafficking, female genital mutilation, serious injury and death. In fact, violence against women has been found to be the most significant contributor to illness, injury and preventable death in women between the ages of 15 and 44 and between 18 and 44 in Victoria, Australia.

More broadly, women—and their children—may experience poverty, homelessness, loss of employment and therefore income and loss of contact with family members and connection with community. The costs to the community of violence against women are enormous and have been estimated at A$13.6 billion rising to A$15.6 billion per annum by 2021 in Australia (National Council 2009); at more than US$5.8 billion each year in the United States (National Center for Injury Prevention and Control 2003) and at £15.7 billion a year in the United Kingdom (Walby 2009). Whilst this research has estimated a financial cost of gender-based violence against women, there are other costs too. These include health-based costs; police, legal and justice system costs; costs in providing crisis accommodation and services and days of absenteeism from work.

In the light of all this information, the importance of taking a broad critical feminist understanding with an intersectional perspective into our practice with women who have experienced gender-based violence is further underscored. (See Chap. 3 for ideas regarding the use of critical feminist theoretical understandings of violence and depression experienced by women). Practitioners require a comprehensive knowledge of the meanings, incidents and impacts of gender-based violence against women, so they are clear in their focus when working with women and capable of explaining to women the dynamics and impacts, including the emotional impacts, of the violence they have experienced.

Contributing Factors to Gender-based Violence Against Women

Despite its severity and prevalence, violence against women is preventable, particularly when addressed within the context of a human rights framework and with multi-level strategies across legal, health, education and other sectors (VicHealth 2004). Contemporary research has revealed a complex interaction of contributing factors to violence against women. One of the most influential determinants of gender-based violence against women is the unequal distribution of resources and power between women and men. This often results from conventional and rigid attitudes to the position of men and women in society. Individuals and communities holding these attitudes tend to consider men as superior to women and that the role of men in the family and in the community is to have the power to make decisions about their livelihoods and the ways in which the family functions. In this instance, men typically have economic and social power and resources as they have the freedom to engage in employment and education and participate in the community. In contrast, women are expected to be amenable and to follow the expectations of males in their family and/or community. Access to education, health care, income and political representation are often curtailed for women in these circumstances (World Health Organisation 2010).

These attitudes and beliefs, whilst sounding outmoded, continue to exist although they are often not overt or acknowledged. For example, there typically remains an economic differential between men and women because even in wealthy countries, men are frequently paid more than women for performing the same work (Corbett and Hill 2012; EOWWA 2012). In Chap. 3, I posed the question, why is gender important? This discrepancy in income between men and women provides another example of the importance of practitioners holding an awareness of gender differences in order to have a comprehensive and contemporary understanding of contributing factors to violence against women. On the face of it, we may think there is no link between different income levels and gender-based violence against women. However, women may be at increased risk of violence when they do not have access to financial security to support themselves and their children or to make decisions about how they might live their lives. Additionally, women have fewer choices to leave or manage a violent domestic situation if they do not have access to independent financial support. The incorporation of an intersectional perspective in critical feminist understandings of violence against women enables practitioners to take a holistic and inclusive view of each woman's situation. It also informs the ways in which feminist groups may be developed and facilitated. The importance of achieving global gender equality as one strategy in the effort to reduce and eliminate gender-based violence against women is evident.

Further, beliefs in, and adherence to, rigidly defined gender roles and stereotypes for women and men may be expressed on individual, social, cultural, community and institutional levels and may include beliefs that what happens within a family is that family's personal concern and responsibility. Cultural attitudes may hold that violence is an acceptable means to resolve conflict and that the use of violence and control against women are acceptable actions to maintain the social order.

As practitioners with women who have experienced gender-based violence, it is crucial for us to have an awareness and understanding of the beliefs and attitudes that can contribute to the occurrence of violence against women. This knowledge will assist us in planning journalling, reflection and discussion activities for feminist group work and providing direction for therapeutic responses. Given the entrenched nature of many traditional and conservative attitudes towards gender-based violence against women and to gender equality in communities, as practitioners we also need to be aware that women, themselves, may hold the same attitudes as those held in their community more generally. They may not even be aware of the attitudes and beliefs they hold. Activities, underpinned by consciousness-raising principles within feminist group work, can assist women to gain a different and deeper understanding of the role that conservative attitudes towards women and gender-based violence against women can play.

The concept of gender, both one's own gender and one's views on gender roles and sexual norms, is closely linked to attitudes to violence against women. Men are more likely than women to hold narrow definitions of behaviours that constitute violence against women, more accepting of excuses for this violence and to hold conservative attitudes towards and accept myths about gender-based violence against women (AIC, SRC and VicHealth 2009; Flood and Pease 2009).

However, community attitudes to gender equality and gender equity are even more influential predictors of attitudes towards gender-based violence against women. Attitudes within peer groups and social networks are persuasive in shaping attitudes towards gender equality as attitudes towards women held by those in organisations such as sporting clubs and religious institutions. Cultural factors play a role in individual and community attitudes towards gender-based violence against women and do vary across cultures, ethnicities and religions (Uthman et al. 2009). Clearly, societal factors such as the use and regulation of the mass media, advertising and pornography also influence attitudes towards women, violence and gender equality.

A related determinant revolves around the existence of, and support for, weak or unenforced sanctions against gender-based violence against women and gender inequality which may be expressed through one or all of individual, social, cultural and institutional levels (VicHealth 2007; World Health Organisation 2009).

An ecological framework within a public health perspective is commonly employed to illustrate and explain, not only the different levels at which violence against women may occur and what factors might contribute to its occurrence, but the different levels on which we need to consider intervening, whether this be through response and/or preventative activities. Briefly, ecological frameworks consist of three or four intersecting levels: the individual and relationship levels; community/organisational level and societal level (Heise 1998; VicHealth 2007; WHO 2002). For example, attitudinal support for violence against women, (that in some instances it is acceptable to use violence against women), may be held by individuals; that is, at the individual and/or relationship level. Strong support for the privacy of the family may be a belief and practice that enables violence against women to occur and is visible at the individual/relationship and at the community/ organisational levels. Weak and unenforceable sanctions against behaviours and practices that enable and reinforce gender inequality, and thus contribute to an environment in which violence against women can occur can be located on the societal level. The ecological framework may be a useful resource to employ with women when attempting to make sense of why gender-based violence against women occurs.

Conclusion

The concepts and issues raised in this chapter can be employed to inform the development of activities for women within feminist support groups including the Women's Journalling Group Programme. These activities would assist women to understand more about their experiences of violence, and as consciousness-raising activities could encourage women to locate responsibility for violence with the perpetrator and to see the reduction and elimination of gender-based violence against women as a community-wide responsibility.

References

Ammar N, Orloff L, Dutton M, Hass G (2012) Battered immigrant women in the United States and protection orders: an exploratory research. Crim Justice Rev 37:337

Anitha S (2011) Legislating gender inequalities: the nature and patterns of domestic violence experienced by south Asian women with insecure immigration status in the United Kingdom. Violence Against Women 17(10):1260–1285

Australian Institute of Criminology, The Social Research Centre and VicHealth (2009) National survey on community attitudes to violence against women 2009: changing cultures, changing attitudes—preventing violence against women: a summary of findings. Victorian Health Promotion Foundation, Melbourne

B.C. Government (2005) Researched to death: B.C. aboriginal women and violence. B.C. Women's Hospital and Health Centre

Corbett C, Hill C (2012) Graduating to a pay gap: the earnings of women and men one year after college graduation. American Association of University Women, Washington DC

Cripps K, Davis M (2012) Communities working to reduce indigenous family violence. Indigenous Justice Clearinghouse, Sydney

Department of Planning and Community Development (2008) Strong culture, strong peoples, strong families: towards a safer future for indigenous families and communities. Department of Planning and Community Development, Melbourne

Duncan J, Western D (2011) Addressing 'the ultimate insult': responding to women experiencing intimate partner sexual violence. University of New South Wales. Australian Domestic and Family Violence Clearinghouse, Sydney

Equal Opportunity for Women in the Workplace Agency (2012) Gender pay gap Australian Government

Family Violence Protection Act (2008) State Of Victoria, Melbourne. http://www.legislation.vic. gov.au/Domino/Web_Notes/LDMS/PubStatbook.nsf/f932b66241ecf1b7ca256e92000e23be/ 083D69EC540CD748CA2574CD0015E27C/$FILE/08-52a.pdf. Accessed 12 Dec 2012

Flood M, Pease B (2009) Factors influencing attitudes to violence against women. Trauma Violence Abuse 10(2):125–142

Fourth World Conference on Women (1995) Beijing platform for action, United Nations division for the advancement of women, Department of Economic And Social Affairs. United Nations, Geneva

Healey L, Howe K, Humphreys C, Jennings C, Julian F (2008) Building the evidence: report on the status of policy and practice in responding to violence against women with disabilities in Victoria. Victorian Women with Disabilities Network Advocacy Information Service, Melbourne

Heise L (1998) Violence against women: an integrated, ecological framework. Violence Against Women 4(3):262–290

Lacey K, McPherson M, Samuel P, Sears K, Head D (2013) The impact of different types of intimate partner violence on the mental and physical health of women in different ethnic groups. J Interpers Violence 28:359

Mouzos J, Makkai T (2004) Women's experiences of male violence: findings from the Australian component of the international violence against women survey (IVAWS). Canberra: Australian Institute of Criminology, Research and Public Policy Series, No. 56

National Center for Injury Prevention and Control (2003) Costs of intimate partner violence against women in the United States. Centers for Disease Control and Prevention, Atlanta

National Clearinghouse on Family Violence (2008) Aboriginal women and family violence. Public Health Agency of Canada, Ottawa

National Council to Reduce Violence Against Women and their Children (2009) The cost of violence against women and their children. Commonwealth of Australia, Canberra

United Nations Declaration on the Elimination of Violence Against Women (1993) http:// www.un-documents.net/a48r104.htm. Accessed 10 Dec 2012

Uthman OA, Lawoko S, Moradi T (2009) Factors associated with attitudes towards intimate partner violence against women: a comparative analysis of 17 sub-Saharan countries. BMC Int Health Hum Rights 9(14)

VicHealth (2004) The health costs of violence: measuring the burden of disease caused by intimate partner violence. Victorian Health Promotion Foundation, Melbourne

VicHealth (2007) Preventing violence before it occurs: a framework and background paper to guide the primary prevention of violence against women in Victoria. Victorian Health Promotion Foundation, Melbourne

Walby S (2009) The cost of domestic violence: up-date 2009 project of the UNESCO chair in gender research. Lancaster University, Leeds

World Health Organisation (2002) World report on violence and health. World Health Organisation, Geneva

World Health Organisation (2005) WHO multi-country study on women's health and domestic violence against women: summary report of initial results on prevalence, health outcomes and women's responses. Geneva, World Health Organization

World Health Organisation (2009) Promoting gender equality to prevent violence against women. World Health Organisation, Geneva

World Health Organisation (2010) Preventing intimate partner and sexual violence against women: taking action and generating evidence. World Health Organisation, Geneva

Chapter 5
Depression in Women

Abstract This chapter explores the nature and incidence of depression in women. A brief overview of various perspectives that theorise depression in women is provided. A critical feminist and gendered understanding, incorporating the concept of intersectionality, has been employed in the previous chapters to analyse and understand gender-based violence against women and to provide a guide and basis for the development and facilitation of a feminist support group for women who have experienced violence and depression. A critical feminist and gendered understanding, incorporating the concept of intersectionality, is now employed to analyse and inform the understanding of depression in women.

Keywords Depression · Gender · Mental health · Recovery · Violence against women · Theoretical understandings of depression · The notion of self

Depression in Women

Depression in women is a gendered mental health problem given that more women than men are likely to experience some form of depression throughout their lifetime. Many factors contribute to the development of depression in women. Many factors also contribute to the ways in which different women perceive and understand the notion of depression and their own experiences that are attributable to depression.

As you read this chapter, it would be useful to keep in mind the concepts and understandings that were raised in Chap. 4 in relation to gender-based violence against women. In particular think about how these concepts and understandings interact with, differ from and/or parallel the concepts, understandings and dynamics that influence and surround depression in women. The connections between gender-based violence against women and depression in women were noted in Chap. 3.

D. Western, *Gender-based Violence and Depression in Women*,
SpringerBriefs in Social Work, DOI: 10.1007/978-1-4614-7532-3_5,
© The Author(s) 2013

The Nature and Incidence of Depression in Women

It is likely that depression is often undiagnosed or underdiagnosed because women do not attend services where diagnosis occurs or will not fully disclose the nature of their health concerns. Consequently the prevalence, frequency and nature of depression experienced by women worldwide can only be estimated. However, the World Health Organisation (2012) has estimated that worldwide, 350 million people may experience depression. It has predicted that depression will be the second most debilitating human condition and contributor to the global burden of disease for all ages and both sexes by 2020 (WHO 2009). Women are twice as likely as men to experience depression and approximately 20 % of women, are likely to experience depression at some time in their lives (Kuehner 2003; Ussher 2010; WHO 2012).

Depression varies in its nature, symptoms and severity. The depressed state often features flat affect, loss of interest in usual activities, low self-esteem, difficulties with concentration and remembering, social withdrawal, changes in day to day activities such as eating and sleeping, and feelings of hopelessness. Depression may be experienced as part of Post-Traumatic Stress Disorder or in response to a complicated grieving process. It may be a component of bi-polar disorder which can vary in severity amongst people depending upon how well medication is managed and used, or it may be triggered following the birth of a child and range from 'the blues' to severe psychosis.

Measures of depression vary and include self-report through to diagnosis based on the Diagnostic and Statistical Manual (DSM-IV; [DSM-V from May 2013]). The DSM-IV-TR, its predecessors and formal biomedical diagnostic procedures have been criticised by feminist researchers and practitioners for the medicalisation and pathologising of depression in women that these procedures engender, not only for women themselves, but for community understandings of women's experiences of depression (Eriksen and Kress 2008; Marecek 2006). As Stoppard and Scattolon (1999) point out, women do not always have access to, nor wish to access, general practitioners, psychologists and/or psychiatrists who provide such diagnoses and consequent treatment, which often takes the form of medication. Prescription of medication or depression is another gendered phenomenon; medication is more often prescribed for women than it is for men. Further, the DSM provides no insight into gendered differences in the experience or frequency of depression.

How Might We Understand Depression in Women and Women's Experiences of Depression?

Giving consideration to factors and stressors associated with women's gendered roles and experiences, as well as influential intersecting factors such as race, socio-economic status, age and (dis)ability (see Chap. 3), provides the opportunity to understand depression in women from a far broader perspective than when exploring women's experiences of depression from single, unconnected theories or perspectives. For instance, not all women living with psychosocial stressors such as parenting young children and simultaneously caring for elderly parents develop depression. How might we, as social work and welfare practitioners, understand the differences amongst women and use this knowledge to inform our practice?

Broad critical perspectives (Morley and Macfarlane 2012; Mullaly 2007) are required in order to thoroughly inform, analyse, respond to and prevent depression in women. A critical feminist perspective holds that the personal is political, that diversity amongst women—and their experiences—must be recognised, that transformation and change on individual and/or societal levels provide foci for social work with women and that contexts and locations in which women are situated are constantly changing. Further, responsibility for understanding and preventing the development and unquestioned attributions, assumptions, expectations and discourses of depression in women must be a multi factorial, multi-level societal commitment. This responsibility and obligation parallels that required for responding to and preventing gender-based violence against women.

Before further exploring a critical feminist and gendered understanding of depression in women, I will look at a number of other explanations and perspectives.

Biological and Biomedical Explanations of Depression in Women

These explanations focus on the roles that women's bodies, reproductive functions and hormonal influences play in the development of depression. These explanations were developed, at least in part, in response to the higher rates of depression in women compared with the rates of depression in men. Hence, diagnoses of premenstrual syndrome, post-partum depression and menopausal mood changes were developed (Ussher 2010). Whilst these experiences of depression for women are very real, a psychiatric diagnosis naming such experiences as disorders, potentially stigmatises and distorts physical processes. Ussher (2010) suggests the concept of a 'critical-realist' epistemology be integrated with other structural and critical feminist theorisings and understandings of the contributing factors to depression in women. A critical-realist epistemology reminds us that, whilst biomedical descriptions and explanations of depression in women can be limited, the lived experiences of depression for women can be highly distressing, confusing, debilitating and physically incapacitating. Ussher (2010) also makes the important point that in order for us to most fully understand the experiences of women with depression, different layers of analysis need to be incorporated rather than privileged one over another.

Lafrance (2007) suggests that biomedical understandings and approaches to depression in women continue to be accepted and maintained in society because of the power that discourses of medicine have to influence the ways in which we understand the world. When we solely seek to understand depression in women through a biomedical lens, we give up the opportunity to gain a comprehensive, multi-faceted understanding and by doing so, depoliticise the occurrence of depression in women and women's subsequent experiences. These considerations are important to bear in mind when we look at the concepts of consciousness-raising and resistance that are a component of the women's journaling groups. I look at these concepts in Chap. 6.

Psychological and Cognitive Explanations

Theories about the impact of women's psychological characteristics suggest differences between women and men in their cognitive styles and the consequent impact this has on the development of depression in women. Women are considered more emotional and ruminative in their thinking and coping styles, whereas men are deemed more likely to take action and to distract themselves from problematic situations (Ussher 2010).

Biomedical and psychological theories generally fail to accommodate a critical feminist or gendered understanding of depression in women. Because explanations of depression in these theories are generally centred within the individual, conflicts for the individual may arise when striving for recovery. For example, women may feel relieved that the reason for their depression is out of their control and not their fault because it is due to faulty chemical interactions in the brain. However, at the same time, women must then deal with the apparent alternative that there is something wrong with them physically; that, as Stoppard (1997, p. 17) writes, "… the possibility that her body, in some unclear and essentially mysterious way, is dysfunctional".

Relational and Psychosocial Stressor Explanations

Relational and psychosocial stressor explanations are closely connected to psychological and cognitive explanations. Commonly, the relational and psychosocial explanations posit that psychosocial and economic stresses may develop from women's experiences of their social roles, the expectations from society (and themselves) about successfully performing (traditional and sometimes stereotyped) women's roles and responsibilities, the impact of gender-based violence in child and adulthood, poverty, single parenting, general violence, harassment and discrimination (Clarke 2006; Kuehner 2003). Women, compared with men, may also be more likely to have lower status jobs, to experience more role strain and be the carers of children, elderly parents and other relatives. These theories suggest that when some or all of these factors also interact with women's sex role socialisation, the development of depression in women is not surprising. By giving consideration to the changes in these factors that women may experience over the course of their lives, a developmental and life stage perspective is introduced.

Early theorists suggested that the presence of positive, mutual, caring relationships where women feel a sense of connection to other people and can develop and maintain a sense of their own identity, are likely to mitigate the occurrence of depression (Jordan et al. 1991). However, in the event that women are engaged in relationships that do not provide this support or care, they could be at risk of developing depression. This risk was expected to increase when women were in relationships characterised by stereotypical female and male attributes where, for example, women are expected to be passive and dependent, men are expected to be dominant and assertive. More recent research, as presented in Chaps. 3 and 4, does indeed show connections between women's experiences of gender-based violence from intimate partners, conservative and stereotypical attitudes to gender equality and the development of mental health illnesses including depression.

Jack (1991, 1999), Jack and Ali (2010) introduced the idea of 'silencing the self' to explain the development and incidence of depression in women. According to Jack, in order to create and maintain social relationships that are important to them, many women attempt to avoid confrontation or disruptions that threaten these relationships. Self-silencing is stipulated by social and cultural norms, values and beliefs that value women's passivity, their caring of others and their selflessness. Consequently, women refrain from seeking to have their needs met and from holding and representing their own views and beliefs. The resultant impact on women's sense of self and identity, as well as on their ability to share their thoughts and feelings, is significant. As Ali et al. (2003, p. 670) write, "This silencing can precipitate an internal self-negation through progressive devaluation of one's own beliefs and ideas. Self-silencing has been found to correlate significantly with depressive symptomatology in various community samples of women". Women are more likely to experience depression as the importance of the relationship to them grows. Because of their desire that these relationships continue over time, women are more likely to restrict and contain their ideas, opinions and needs. Women whose primary source of sense of self comes from non-relational domains such as career, exercise or spirituality, are less likely to 'self-silence'. A consideration to bear in mind with relational explanations is that they do not always pay adequate attention to structural and systemic factors and contexts and their impacts on women and on the development of depression in women.

A Feminist Social Constructionist Understanding of Depression in Women

Stoppard (2000) argues for a feminist social constructionist understanding of depression in women that comes from a material—discursive perspective; that is, one that takes into account notions of corporeal, psychosocial, psychological and subjective, lived experiences and locations of women and how these contribute to the development of self and the development of depression. Such an understanding removes the either/or choice of the biomedical, physical, psychosocial and psychological explanations imposed by the ostensibly separate and unconnected theories that I presented above. A feminist social constructionist understanding also provides space where women's own accounts of their depression experiences can be told.

Critical Feminist Theoretical Perspectives and Explanations About Depression in Women

In addition to considering biological, medical, relational and psychological perspectives, critical feminist perspectives explore the role that gender plays in the development of depression in women. As with understanding gender-based violence against women, the inclusion of gender as a contributing factor to women's experiences of depression is crucial.

As a result of the power of gender influences and discourses, a critical feminist perspective seeks to understand depression in women by examining women's experiences across a range of backgrounds including biological, social, cultural, relational, structural, economic, political and psychological contexts. When we add the concept of intersectionality, as discussed in Chap. 3, a critical feminist understanding will also encourage us to think about factors that intersect with gender such as race and ethnicity, age, class and sexuality. This understanding of depression in women enables the holding of perspectives that look beyond the individual facets of women's lives and, therefore, can remove the risk of holding women accountable and responsible for the development and experience of their depression.

By thinking about women's experiences of depression using these different viewpoints, a wide-ranging, yet intricate and highly informed understanding of depression in women can be gained. For example, when working with elderly women, how might we understand their experiences of violence and depression given not only their gender, but their age and class? Possible insights arise when we think about how elderly women might perceive their options when they have a violent partner. Older women may believe very strongly in staying with their partner irrespective of the ways in which they are treated. For many older women, leaving a relationship may mean they leave their home of many years, face financial hardship and become isolated from friends and other supports they have had over their lifetime. Another practice example may ask the question: How might we understand the experiences of violence and depression when we work with Aboriginal and indigenous women? Gender is important, but so too are race, racism, culture and socio-economic status and the way these factors intersect. When we understand that much of the violence against indigenous women occurs due to the impacts of colonialism—dispossession of land, historical violence toward indigenous peoples, loss of culture, language, traditional gender roles and social structures, removal of indigenous children from their families, a sense of powerlessness and social dislocation—we begin to develop a multi-faceted, comprehensive understanding (Cripps and Davis 2012; Department of Human Services 2012; Dylan et al. 2008). This understanding will then inform the ways in which we work with indigenous women—and the ways in which we might structure and facilitate a feminist group work response in the form of a women's journaling group. A useful question to ask ourselves as practitioners is: What factors in women's experiences of violence and depression might we need to consider in order to develop journaling and group activities that are relevant, non-judgemental and that inspire and encourage women to redevelop their self-confidence and achieve the changes they would like to pursue in their lives?

In addition, it is crucial to seek out and to hear women's own accounts of their experiences of depression as these can then accurately inform practitioners' understandings of the ways in which women experience depression and the impacts it has on their lives. Reflecting solid feminist social work practice, the process of seeking women's accounts of their experiences and the sense they make of these experiences, opens the relationship between social workers and women. Women can become active partners in the therapeutic processes within feminist group work.

The Notion of Self in Understanding Women's Experiences of Depression

The notion of self is central to understanding the development and impact of depression in women. What has constituted one's understanding of 'self' through time has depended upon one's epistemological and theoretical viewpoints. From a feminist critical perspective, the self is composed of the physical body as well as the emotional, spiritual, psychological and intellectual elements within each woman (Cameron and McDermott 2007; Ussher 1997). Moreover, one is less likely to have a unified self, than to have multiple, changing and evolving selves and identities (or subjectivities) that adapt to, and are influenced by, the contexts in which women live (Qin 2004; Stapleton 2000). Historical, social, political, legal, cultural and economic contexts which are, of course, themselves always shifting and changing result in differences between women in the selves that they experience and hold as women. Thus, within critical feminist theorising around gender-based violence against women and depression in women, differences amongst women are acknowledged and appreciated. The impact of differential contexts and power relations also mean, however, that women can be inhibited and restricted when developing and changing their senses of self and identity. Lafrance and Stoppard (2006), for example, found that women with depression commonly described their self-identities in terms of their gendered roles and their efforts to meet social expectations. The descriptor 'good' was regularly combined with a female identity such as girl, wife and mother; the result being the creation of the 'good woman' identity within societal "discourses of femininity" (Stoppard 2000, p. 106).

Finding that women sought to discover different ways to reject and discard the 'good woman' role, Lafrance and Stoppard (2006, p. 316) note "… the good woman is constructed as a false identity which restrains and constricts a woman's authentic self". Thus, the concepts of authentic and false selves become relevant in thinking about how depression might develop in women and how women might perceive and understand their experiences and recovery processes.

Much has been written about the concepts of authentic and false selves. Goffman (1959) wrote of the performing self that we enact and demonstrate according to the way we think others expect us to behave and/or the ways in which we desire them to see us. Sincere performers believe in the self and impression they present, whilst cynical performers do not believe in the act they perform, although they may continue to enact their role if they believe it benefits those around them. Winnicott (1965) theorised that true and false selves develop early in infancy and that a false self develops when necessary in order to protect and hide one's true self. Winnicott (1965) maintained this is likely to occur when the spontaneity and creativity of the true self and, thus, the inner reality of the infant, is unable to develop in a safe and predictable fashion. The false self, which is characterised by compliance to social and environmental demands and expectations, takes over from the true self. As the infant develops, so too does the false self along with relationships based around the false self. The true self, however, could remain, be acknowledged, and when safe, be repatriated into one's overall self, albeit over a long period of time and with intensive support and/or therapy.

These theories mirror the notion of the role of the 'good woman' enacted by women who focus on the needs of others with little or no consideration of their own needs. Although women with depression may not identify themselves as cynical performers, understanding the development of depression as a possible result of consistently performing an inauthentic role, or performing as the false self, may provide them with an opportunity to stop engaging in their roles, to gain an understanding of how their depression might have developed, and to reassess their sense of self and identity.

Most of the women who participated in my research felt, at times, constrained and captured by roles, expectations, assumptions and beliefs that shaped their whole, rather than parts of, their identity. This sense of limitation was experienced in spite of advantages such as close relationships, financial security, and life meaning that attended some of these roles. Even when the women acknowledged that they had made an active decision, a choice, in the roles they took on, this acknowledgement did not diminish the feeling of lack of true identity and of conforming. Jessica described this as a result of "All that stuff that you do because you have to and someone needs you to and all that kind of thing". She also disclosed that "(This) has just been a huge struggle because I don't fit that shape very well. And so for me, I guess when I really feel that I'm having to conform to the traditional stereotype, I find that really hard because that's not who I am".

Naomi added "So again, the no voice; you don't discuss it because it's not appropriate or not the ladylike thing to do. You know, it all builds up".

When considering facilitating a feminist group work response through a women's journaling group, holding an awareness of the links between women's senses of self and identity on the one hand and women's recovery processes and experiences on the other helps inform the development of therapeutic journaling activities and group work agendas.

Women and Recovery from Depression:
Ideas About Recovery

Discussion and debate about the most effective pharmacotherapy and psychotherapy responses for depression experienced by women is characterised by extensive and different viewpoints, often from contrasting and conflicting positions. I will not explore these responses other than to note that medication and the provision of counselling (often cognitive-behavioural approaches and interpersonal therapy) are commonly offered to women. In general, however, most research has found that for mild to moderate depressions, psychotherapies may be sufficient intervention. For more severe depression, and for chronic or recurrent depression, recommendations are usually made for a combination of drug therapy and psychotherapy (Cuijpers et al. 2012; Friedman and Clancy 2003).

Given the uncertainty of any one, or even combination of approaches, in successfully treating depression and the need for further research in relation to most therapeutic interventions, a feminist group work response with a women's journaling group might offer another alternative to psychotherapy and an alternative that women can use on their own or in conjunction with other interventions. These possibilities are explored further in Chaps. 8, 9 and 10.

Contemporary understandings of recovery from mental illness stress that individuals benefit from determining their own meanings of, and milestones toward, recovery. This enables women to have some level of input, decision and control over the ways in which they manage and recover from depression. Recovery from mental illness need not mean a return to women's pre-depression living style and/or level of functioning (Ramon et al. 2007). Indeed, for many women, such a return is not possible given that the process of recovery can be lengthy during which time considerable changes may have occurred in both the woman and her surrounding milieu.

Researchers like O'Brien and Fullagar (2008) report that, as a part of recovering from depression, many women see a need to integrate the depression they have experienced into their lives; that it becomes a part of who they are and that they can still live fulfilling and satisfying lives. Women in my research also spoke about the need to sometimes sit with depression for a period of introspection during which they could sometimes find a deeper understanding of themselves and of what the depression might signify about the ways in which they were living their lives. Jessica, for example, reflected, "I get very bored with myself when I'm like that. But it's almost like I have to do that before I've got the energy to move forward". Phoebe's experience of depression and recovery was similar: "I think I have to feel the pain and be in it before I can come out to talk about it. And I can only do that in my own space". The process of recovery is clearly nonlinear, multi-directional and the process is as important as the outcome.

Factors that can be crucial in assisting women in their recovery from depression include the ability and capacity of women to make choices about their recovery processes and directions; the importance of hope and encouragement in the process (Houghton 2007); connection with others; active involvement in community whether this is through social, creative, educational or occupational activities; and the strengthening of self-esteem, self-confidence, and a sense of control over one's life and wellbeing (Mancini 2007; Meehan et al. 2008; Ralph 2000; Ramon et al. 2007). Integrating these factors into journaling, discussion and reflection activities within women's journaling groups provides each woman with opportunities to think about the ways in which these factors may be relevant to them.

Finally, it is worth noting that a gendered understanding of women's recovery from depression is not commonly evident in these recent recovery approaches (O'Brien and Fullagar 2008). For those women where a focus on their 'self' is barely considered and where uncertainty about themselves and their identities underlie their depression, there is risk that they can feel further disempowered, ineffective, culpable and to have failed again if they believe they are not recovering in the ways, or the speed at which they think others expect from them (O'Brien 2012). When developing journaling and group activities, practitioners must be cognisant of this.

Conclusion

This chapter has explored the nature and prevalence of depression in women throughout the world. A number of theories, explanations and perspectives that have been developed to assist in understanding depression in women and recovery processes were discussed. Concepts such as that of the 'self' that have been important in understanding the development of depression in women and women's experiences of depression and recovery were introduced. A gendered and critical feminist theoretical understanding incorporating the concept of intersectionality was employed in order to provide a comprehensive and fully informed foundation for understanding and analysing the presence of depression in women. This foundation will be used in the presentation of a feminist group work response, through a women's journaling group, for women who have experienced gender-based violence and subsequent depression.

References

Ali A, Oatley K, Toner B (2003) Life stress, self-silencing, and domains of meaning in unipolar depression: an investigation of an outpatient sample of women. J Soc Clin Psychol 21(6):669–685

Cameron N, McDermott F (2007) Social work and the body. New York Palgrave MacMillan

Clarke, H. 2006. Depression: women's sadness or high-prevalence disorder? Aust Social Work 59(4):365–377

Cripps K, Davis M (2012) Communities working to reduce Indigenous family violence. Brief 12. Indigenous Justice Clearinghouse, Sydney

Cuijpers P, Reynolds C, Donker T, Juan L, Andersson G, Beekman A (2012) Personalized treatment of adult depression: medication, psychotherapy, or both? A systematic review. Depression Anxiety 29(10):855–864

Department of Human Services (2012) Indigenous family violence primary prevention framework. State of Victoria, Melbourne

Dylan A, Regehr C, Alaggia R (2008) And justice for all? Aboriginal victims of sexual violence. Violence Against Women 14(6):678–696

Eriksen K, Kress V (2008) Gender and diagnosis: struggles and suggestions for counsellors. J Couns Dev 86:152–162

Friedman R, Clancy C (2003) The evaluation and management of depression in primary care: an evidence-based review, part 2: Treatment. J Clin Outcomes Manag 10(2):104–118

Goffman E (1959) The presentation of self in everyday life. Penguin, Harmondsworth

Houghton S (2007) Exploring hope: its meaning for adults living with depression and for social work practice. Aust J Adv Mental Health, 6(3):186–193. http://search.informit.com.au/documentSummary;dn=477079577708973;res=IELHEA ISSN: 1446–7984

Jack D (1991) Silencing the self: women and depression. Harvard University Press, Cambridge

Jack D (1999) Silencing the self: inner dialogues and outer realities. In: Joiner T, Coyne J (eds) The interactional nature of depression: advances in interpersonal approaches. American Psychological Association, Washington DC, pp 221–246

Jack D, Ali A (2010) Silencing the self across cultures: depression and gender in the social world. Oxford University Press, Oxford

Jordan J, Kaplan A, Miller J, Stiver I, Surrey J (1991) Women's growth in connection: writings from the Stone Centre. Guilford, New York

Kuehner C (2003) Gender differences in unipolar depression: an update of epidemiological findings and possible explanations. Acta Psychiatr Scand 108:163–174

Lafrance M (2007) A bitter pill: a discursive analysis of women's medicalized accounts of depression. J Health Psychol 12(1):127–140

Lafrance M, Stoppard J (2006) Constructing a non-depressed self: women's accounts of recovery from depression. Feminism Psychol 16(3):307–324

Mancini M (2007) The role of self-efficacy in recovery from serious psychiatric disabilities. Qual Soc Work 6(1):49–74

Marecek J (2006) Social suffering, gender, and women's depression. In: Keyes C, Goodman S (eds) Women and depression: a handbook for the social, behavioural and biomedical sciences. Cambridge University Press, Cambridge

Meehan T, King R, Beavis P, Robinson J (2008) Recovery-based practice: do we know what we mean or mean what we know? Aust N Z J Psychiatry 42:177–182

Morley C, Macfarlane S (2012) The Nexus between Feminism and Postmodernism: still a central concern for critical social work. British J Soc Work 42:687–705

Mullaly B (2007) The new structural social work, 3rd edn. Oxford University Press, Don Mills

O'Brien W (2012) The recovery imperative: a critical examination of mid-life women's recovery from depression. Soc Sci Med 75:573–580

O'Brien W, Fullagar S (2008) Rethinking the relapse cycle of depression and recovery: a qualitative investigation of women's experiences. Soc Altern 27(4):6–13

Qin D (2004) Toward a critical feminist perspective of culture and self. Feminism Psychol 14(2):297–312

Ralph R (2000) Review of recovery literature: a synthesis of a sample of recovery literature 2000. National Technical Assistance Centre for State Mental Health Planning, Maine

Ramon S, Healy B, Renouf N (2007) Recovery from mental illness as an emergent concept and practice in Australia and the UK. Int J Soc Psychiatry 53:108

Stapleton K (2000) 1. In search of the self: feminism, postmodernism and identity. Feminism Psychol 10(4):463–469

Stoppard J (1997) Women's bodies, women's lives and depression: towards a reconciliation of material and discursive accounts. In: Ussher J (ed) Body talk: the material and discursive regulation of sexuality, madness and reproduction. Routledge, London

Stoppard J (2000) Understanding depression: feminist social constructionist approaches. Routledge, London

Stoppard J, Scattolon Y (1999) "Getting on with life": women's experiences and ways of coping with depression. Can Psychol 40(2):205

Ussher J (1997) Introduction: towards a material-discursive analysis of madness, sexuality and reproduction. In: Ussher J (ed) Body talk: the material and discursive regulation of sexuality, madness and reproduction. Routledge, London

Ussher J (2010) Are we medicalising women's misery? A critical review of women's higher rates of reported depression. Feminism Psychol 20(1):9–35

Winnicott DW (1965) Ego distortion in terms of true and false self. In: Winnicott DW (ed) The maturational processes and the facilitating environment: studies in the theory of emotional development. The Hogarth Press Limited, London

World Health Organisation (2009) Depression: World Health Organisation. World Health Organisation, Geneva

World Health Organisation (2012) Depression: Fact Sheet no. 369. World Health Organisation, Geneva

Chapter 6
Feminist Group Work, Consciousness-Raising and Resistance

Abstract In this chapter, I explore feminist group work practice. In doing so I consider two powerful concepts that are typically incorporated into feminist group work practice: consciousness-raising and resistance. I examine the role that consciousness-raising and resistance can play in guiding the development of journaling activities and in guiding the facilitation of women's journaling groups. Why are these concepts important to women's journaling about depression? Why are they important in women's understandings about their experiences of violence and depression? In order to answer these questions, I present the relevant theory and literature that looks at the concepts of consciousness-raising and resistance, the ways they can be employed as methods, as activities themselves, and how they can underpin discussions with women about their rights. Consciousness-raising and resistance methods and activities fit neatly into critical feminist intersectional theories of gender-based violence against women and depression in women, particularly when we think about ways to respond to and prevent violence and depression.

Keywords Consciousness-raising · Resistance · Group work · Feminist group work · Depression · Journaling · Violence against women

Practice Theory and Knowledge: A Critical Feminist Approach to Group Development and Group Structure

Critical feminist group work theory and methodology underpins the Women's Journaling Group Program. Butler and Wintram's (1991, p. 17) explanation of feminist group work is very relevant; "Integrated throughout (the group work process) is the belief that women have the right to seek power and control over their own lives, and to feel secure in challenging conventional images of

D. Western, *Gender-based Violence and Depression in Women*,
SpringerBriefs in Social Work, DOI: 10.1007/978-1-4614-7532-3_6,
© The Author(s) 2013

themselves. The group provides scope for re-evaluation, with change emerging out of collective and individual action".

A number of feminist principles are central to feminist group work and these are embedded within the Women's Journaling Group Program. These principles include the use of a gendered and diversity lens to see, hear and explore the everyday experiences of women and the ways in which social, cultural, political, medical and historical norms and contexts can oppress women in their everyday lives and, consequently, act as factors that contribute to women's depression. The importance of learning from each other through reciprocal support, sharing, connection and different perspectives is another principle within feminist group work. In practising these activities within therapeutic groups, women have opportunities to witness and validate other women's experiences of depression, including their efforts toward recovery. In turn each woman has her own experiences witnessed and validated in a non-judgemental milieu. This mutual aid focus of feminist group work, characterised by reciprocity and collaboration between women, as well as high levels of support and acceptance, offers significant potential for innovative recovery-focused mental health practice (Hyde 2013).

Within feminist groups, considerations are given to possible power imbalances within groups, particularly between facilitator and group members, but also potentially between women members themselves in their abilities to engage and participate within a group. The sharing of life experiences, and of experiences within the group, can be one way to assist all women to feel a sense of belonging, connection and involvement in a group. Incorporating a reflective component into group sessions can also assist as women are given opportunities to reflect on their insights, learnings and participation. These reflections/evaluations can be shared with group members or kept private for each woman. This is a decision group members can make at the beginning of a group.

Group facilitators need to decide for themselves whether, to what extent and how they may share their own personal experiences of depression or violence, for example, and how appropriate this is. Feminist group work practice suggests that, in order to reduce power imbalances, group facilitators do share elements of their life experiences within groups they facilitate.

Traditional group work theory holds that groups move through given stages of development and growth. Tuckman's (1975) five-stage model includes the stages of forming, storming, norming, performing and adjourning (McDermott 2002) whilst Garland et al. (1965) incorporate a similar developmental process in their five stages of pre-affiliation, power and control, intimacy, differentiation and termination. Might there be an alternative way of viewing the development of groups based on feminist understandings of group work in the context of a critical feminist understanding of women and depression?

Schiller (1997) suggests that groups composed of women move through developmental stages in ways that differ from groups of men or of children. Building on the Garland et al. (1965) model, Schiller (1995) introduced the relational model of stages of development in women's groups. Holding a feminist perspective and understanding of women's needs, Schiller (1997) contends that connection and affiliation with others is a primary focus for women, as is their need for a sense of safety in groups and a general sense of discomfort and uncertainty around issues of conflict and power within group and other social settings. Consequently, she proposes that the first and last stages of traditional group theory about group development (pre-affiliation and termination), remain relevant for women's groups, and that the middle stages be replaced with the three stages of establishing a relational base; mutuality and interpersonal empathy; and challenge and change.

Schiller (1997) maintains that this relational model allows for time and space to be given to the building of relationships, connections and understandings between women prior to the surfacing of any issues surrounding difference, disagreement or conflict between them. Women are more likely to introduce new and different ideas or thoughts when they feel they know each other in the group, when they feel safe there and when they feel they can trust the strength, affiliation and longevity of the relationships developed within the group. Addressing issues of power, conflict and challenge at a later stage in the life of the group, also allows women to feel safer about tolerating difference in others and understanding that difference can co-exist with characteristics held in common with other women. When seen in a context of different, but safe, challenges and conflicts can provide productive learning and reflective opportunities for women in groups (Schiller 1997).

Herman (1992), in writing about working with women experiencing traumatic responses, stated that group work could offer support, validation, witness, information and shared experiences for women. She noted "Groups lend a kind of formality and ritual solemnity to individual grief; they help the survivor at once to pay homage to her losses in the past and to repopulate her life in the present" (Herman 1992, p. 228).

Consciousness-Raising

Incorporating many of the principles within feminist group work is the concept of consciousness-raising. This was one of the earliest and most significant activities employed by women within the second wave of feminism in the 1960s and 1970s (MacKinnon 1989; Sowards and Renegar 2006). MacKinnon (1989, p. 83) referred to consciousness-raising as *the* feminist method and defined it as "... the collective critical reconstitution of the meaning of women's social experience, as women live through it". Women, largely in Western societies, joined together to talk about and share their stories and experiences of what it meant to be a woman which included accounts of abortion, sexual harassment, rape, domestic violence and unequal pay and employment opportunities. Women often then identified a second layer of these experiences; oppression, fear, silence, limited choice and decision making opportunities, and a lack of identity and self-concept outside of relationships with other people (MacKinnon 1989). As women spoke and shared their stories and emotions, their consciousness was raised about not only their own situations, but those of other women experiencing similar or the same concerns and restrictions (Dicker and Piepmeier 2003).

There is a strong connection between consciousness-raising and women creating and voicing narratives about themselves and their experiences. This is a two-way process; as women construct narratives about themselves and their experiences of depression and violence, their consciousness is raised. As women's level of consciousness and insight into their experiences and situations is raised, their narratives change and can be redeveloped or whole new ones generated.

The slogan, the 'personal is political' reminds women that what happens in their lives can be seen from a broader, overarching structural and societal level. Each woman's experience of violence and depression is unique. However, because so many women experience gender-based violence and depression, these can be recognised as political concerns and removed from the supposed failures and inadequacies of any one individual woman. With a shared and changed consciousness, greater self-confidence and support from each other, women can reach new understandings and insights into their situations. They can also then make decisions that can alter the ways in which they live their lives; in effect they can resist aspects of their situations that are imposed upon them or that direct how and who they should be as women. This does not mean that women are responsible for stopping violence that is directed against them or that they are responsible for simply 'pulling themselves together' to stop feeling depressed. The use of consciousness-raising and resistance as methods for social work practice and as informants for journaling activities and group facilitation opens up new possibilities for women in the understandings and beliefs—the narratives—they have about themselves and what alternatives they may be able to consider.

The contexts in which consciousness-raising can be used have expanded to focus on the diversity, as well as the similarities, of women's experiences, backgrounds, contexts, characteristics and perspectives (Comerford and Fambrough 2002). In addition, varied activities often made possible through technological advances in social media and communication methods are now considered relevant to consciousness-raising for women (Sowards and Renegar 2004, 2006). Examples of these activities include online blogs, zines, podcasts, social networking sites such as Facebook, everyday informal conversations and interactions, popular culture and media such as films and music, and leadership positions that can be used to advance feminist activism from wherever women are situated.

Feminist activism through consciousness-raising can occur via the activities of women responding and acting individually, not only through traditional collective action. Journaling on an individual basis and/or within a Women's Journaling Group can act as a method of consciousness-raising about the contributing factors to gender-based violence against women and to women's experiences of depression. Feminist activism can also occur through the processes of challenging and resisting gender stereotypes, labels and norms; that is, "A deliberate failing to meet the preconceived notions of patriarchal society" (Sowards and Renegar 2006, p. 68). This activism introduces the idea of resistance. Resistance can involve refusal to undertake expected roles and responsibilities; the questioning and subversion of accepted ways of living, being and conforming to societal values and discourses; and changing one's sense of self and identity in line with one's own desires and needs rather than in response to the needs and desires of others. Resistance delivers change, assertiveness, self-determination and power and control back to the individual woman.

Resistance in Women's Journaling

One of the activities and outcomes within the processes of consciousness-raising is resistance. The notion of resistance refers to the emotions, cognitions and activities in which one engages in order to respond to situations of oppression and unequal power. Women's resistance in journals operates on a micro political level (Mullaly 2002) as they firstly begin to raise their consciousness about their own depression and the factors contributing to its development and continuation over time. I do not use the term 'resistance' in a way that suggests women are victims or that if women do not engage in 'resistant' activities they are content or in some way, too lazy, non-compliant or passive to take action (Convery 2007; Thomas and Davies 2005). A critical feminist intersectional understanding of depression reminds us of the varied contributors to women's depression and the varied barriers and difficulties facing women attempting to recover from depression.

Eschle and Maiguashca (2007, p. 2127) note that critical feminist resistance can be expressed in a range of ways and in different locations. They conclude that "… solidarity and collective identity should be understood as a creative process, rather than an end point, sustained through organisational structures and emotional attachments, and involving the continual contestation of inequality and negotiation of difference". These are activities, processes and dynamics that can occur within feminist based groups such as Women's Journaling Groups.

Thomas and Davies (2005) note that small-scale, routine and less overt forms of critical feminist resistance are as legitimate as large-scale movements because of the ways in which they can still challenge and change not only actions, but meanings and understandings about conformist and conventional ways of being. These forms of resistance centred "… on the destabilizing of truths, challenging subjectivities and normalizing discourses" (Thomas and Davies 2005, p. 720). So, by identifying, questioning and changing dominant social and political discourses through journaling, discussion and reflection, women are enabled to resist the social roles, responsibilities and expectations placed upon them and to remake their identities in ways that more accurately reflect their genuine selves. White (1997, p. 82) observed the possible life changing influence of women's journaling when she wrote: "Through autobiographical texts, women are able to offer their own interpretations and re-evaluations of the power structures that seek to control and silence them. Because the safety of the journal allows women to center (sic) themselves as subjects, journal writing functions as a form of discursive resistance".

In further considering the possibility of such resistance taking place in women's journals, two authors' efforts stand out. Brenner (1997) wrote about women's spiritual and intellectual resistance in her exploration of the writing and journals of four Jewish women at the time of the Holocaust in World War Two. Referring to the writings of Anne Frank, Simone Weil, Edith Stein and Etty Hillesum as autobiographical, Brenner (1997, p. 5) saw the women's "self-introspection as a mode of resistance". The women's resistance centred on their efforts to maintain a sense of awareness, control and hope in a situation that seemed beyond hope and beyond understanding. By retaining their dignity, self-respect, concern for others and faith in a moral world, the women found ways, through their writings, to resist the overwhelming upheavals and threats to their survival. In her research about women's life writing in the face of catastrophic situations such as war, political conflict and other exposure to violence, Fuchs (2004) similarly described the strength, direction and control afforded women through their writing. She also noted the opportunities that writing provided for women to resist and protest oppression and situations that were not of their making and were beyond their control. Rather than accepting a passive role, women, through writing, exercised creativity, reflection and planning in their efforts to rebuild from catastrophe. A significant element of rebuilding revolved around (re)connecting with the self and self-representation.

So, how might women engage in activities of resistance within their journals and within Women's Journaling Groups? Naomi journaled about becoming more assertive: "Letting myself be deserving is one thing but now I need to expect it from others, and myself, and then keep that expectation at a 'deserving' level". Jessica's journaling was similar: "It is ok to challenge; it is ok to speak up. It is ok to acknowledge the other side but invisibility is not an option. Victimhood is not an option". Zoe was clear about resisting and why it was important: "Journaling is part of that resistance. It's saying, I'm not going to do what I should. Giving to yourself at times".

Sowards and Renegar (2006) and Lafrance (2009) found that women often recover from depression when they resist, to one degree or another, the gendered societal stereotypes and myths that place women in the roles of the 'good woman'. Clearly included in these stereotypes is the 'good' woman in her various manifestations of wife, mother, daughter, worker; all roles that although often unspoken and hidden, still frequently constitute the feminine ideal of meaning, purpose and identity (Beauboeuf-Lafontant 2008; Belenky et al. 1997; Lafrance and Stoppard 2006). Penny's journaling describes her frustrations with these expectations: "Expect me to be in control, happy, have it all done, work, housework, budget, good partner, good daughter, good friend, good worker, good mother, good tennis player, good runner. Then I feel overwhelmed, worried and anxious. Being in control of your emotions is a big one, especially the sad or angry emotions. Other people feel uncomfortable about them".

Although the process is quite complex and gradual, women can begin to gain different perspectives and understandings about themselves and their rights when they begin to resist and consider alternatives to:

- Their lack of opportunity to identify and express their emotions, particularly emotions such as anger;
- Their loss of a sense of self, identity and self-value;
- The impact of structural and gendered social roles, relationships and expectations that disable and immobilise their authentic selves and identities;
- The lack of time and space to undertake and reflect on personal growth and accomplishments;
- Limited time out and self-care for themselves, away from their normative roles and expectations.

Resistance to these factors can begin by women's participation in a Women's Journaling Group. Such participation breaks down the isolation of individuals who then share ideas, hopes and desires for changes to their selves and the world around them. Each woman in reflecting on, sharing and talking about her responses to the journaling activities, has opportunities to not only model and practice how she would like to be different, but can experience this process as affirming and acceptable because of validating and encouraging feedback from the other women. One woman's feedback about her participation in a women's journaling group stated that the group "Has reduced my sense of isolation as there are many themes shared by all group members. Has been important to me to voice my voice! I tend to be very quiet and private and in the group because of the shared experience I have felt able to contribute".

Women can further resist factors that contribute to their experiences of depression by naming the activities that bring meaning and purpose to their lives and that sustain them during hard times. Grounding activities such as reconnecting with nature are vital for some women in their resistance and recovery from depression. Fullagar (2008) found that through creative and leisure activities women can transform their sense of self and identity to a stronger sense of their authentic self. Creative activities included journaling and community theatre; actively embodied activities included swimming and strength training; and social activities included visiting friends and attending films. Penny's journaling showed this clearly: "Painting, drawing, scribbling, cutting, pasting. Beach, nature, exploring, bike riding, walking, getting amongst it. Getting in touch with nature and my love for nature; that I'm part of nature and therefore my love for myself. Something that I've been working on to be a part of it and have that link".

In their journaling, women also demonstrate resistance through rehearsal of potential changes and alterations to selves and situations. The existence of realistic and achievable alternatives is crucial for women; finding the balance between hope and reality can be difficult and is a topic that can usefully be raised and explored in women's journaling groups. Having a commitment to making an alternative future a reality (Eschle and Maiguashca 2007, pp. 296–297) is also important and is an area in which social workers may need to support women, particularly at the conclusion of a women's journaling group. Women noted that the following ideas help them to feel hopeful, resist depression and resist the factors that contribute to the development of their depression: taking chances, escaping, freedom, travel, nature, country, religion, faith, choices, cooking, relationships, exercise, confidence, humour, time for reflection, practice expressing emotions and celebration.

Conclusion

Women can engage in processes of consciousness-raising and resistance in order to reach clearer understandings of themselves and their depression and to make choices about their future. Whilst women may not name their journaling and the processes therein as consciousness-raising and resistance, within women's journaling groups they can engage in overt activities such as expressing emotion, asking questions, considering alternatives, making choices and reconfiguring their identities and social roles. These activities differ significantly from the day-to-day activities that emanate from and surround their depression. The opportunity to engage in any form of resistance to depression and to the factors that contribute to the development of depression in women takes the focus away from depression—and violence—as the individual woman's responsibility and something inherent in her disposition. Instead the focus shifts towards a structural and systemic critical feminist understanding and analysis of depression. This is so for women who participate in women's journaling groups and for the practitioners who facilitate and further develop them.

References

Beauboeuf-Lafontant T (2008) Listening past the lies that make us sick: a voice-centred analysis of strength and depression among black women. Qual Sociol 31:391–406

Belenky M, Clinchy B, Goldberger N, Tarule J (1997) Women's ways of knowing. Basic Books, New York

Brenner R (1997) Writing as resistance: four women confronting the Holocaust. Pennsylvania State University Press, Pennsylvania

Butler S, Wintram C (1991) Feminist group work. Sage, London

Comerford S, Fambrough M (2002) Constructing learning sites for solidarity and social action: gender autobiography for consciousness-raising. Affilia 17(4):411–428

Convery A (2007) Resisting "resistance": against a hegemonic trend in feminist theory. Paper presented at the Australasian Political Studies Association conference

Dicker R, Piepmeier A (2003) Introduction. In: Dicker R, Piepmeier A (eds) Catching a wave: reclaiming feminism for the twenty-first century. Northeastern University Press, Boston

Eschle C, Maiguashca B (2007) Rethinking globalised resistance: feminist activism and critical theorising in international relations. Br J Politics Int Relat 9:284–301

Fullagar S (2008) Leisure practices as counter-depressants: emotion-work and emotion-play within women's recovery from depression. Leis Sci 30(1):35–52

Fuchs M (2004) The text is myself: women's life writing and catastrophe. The University of Wisconsin Press, Madison

Garland J, Jones HE, Kolodny R (1965) A model for stages of development in social work groups. In: Bernstein S (ed) Explorations in group work: essays in theory and practice. Charles Rivers Books, Boston

Herman J (1992) Trauma and recovery: from domestic abuse to political terror. Pandora, London

Hyde B (2013) Mutual aid group work: social work leading the way to recovery-focused mental health practice. Soc Work Groups 36(1):43–58

Lafrance M (2009) Women and depression: recovery and resistance. Routledge, London

Lafrance M, Stoppard J (2006) Constructing a non-depressed self: women's accounts of recovery from depression. Fem Psychol 16(3):307–324

MacKinnon C (1989) Toward a feminist theory of the state. Harvard University Press, London

McDermott F (2002) Group work in the mental health field: researching outcome. Aust Soc Work 56(4):352–363

Mullaly B (2002) Challenging oppression: a critical social work approach. Oxford University Press, Oxford

Schiller L (1995) Stages of development in women's groups: a relational model. In: Kurland R, Salmon R (eds) Group work practice in a troubled society. The Haworth Press, New York

Schiller L (1997) Rethinking stages of development in women's groups: implications for practice. Soc Work Groups 20(3):3–19

Sowards S, Renegar V (2004) The rhetorical functions of consciousness-raising in third wave feminism. Commun Stud 55(4):535–552

Sowards S, Renegar V (2006) Reconceptualising rhetorical activism in contemporary feminist contexts. Howard J Commun 17:57–74

Thomas R, Davies A (2005) What have the feminists done for us? feminist theory and organizational resistance. Organization 12(5):711–740

Tuckman, Bruce W (1975) Measuring Educational Outcomes. New York: Harcourt Brace Jovanovich

White L (1997) Silenced stories: may Sarton's journals as a form of discursive resistance. In: Coleman L (ed) Women's life writing: finding voice/building community. Bowling Green State University Popular Press, Bowling Green

Chapter 7
Women and Journaling

Abstract This chapter provides a short introduction to the practice of journaling. I explore the concept of journaling for therapeutic purposes and look briefly at some of the research into the effectiveness and impact of journaling, or at least expressive and therapeutic writing, on mental and physical health. The concept of narratives in therapeutic writing is introduced and some examination of the role that narratives play for women in understanding and recovering from traumatic events such as gender-based violence and mental illness such as depression is undertaken. The rationale for women's journaling and the techniques that can be used are considered.

Keywords Journals · Narratives · Therapeutic writing · Self-development · Diaries · Expressive writing · Depression · Violence against women

Journaling as a Therapeutic Intervention

Journaling, or journal therapy, is the use of writing for therapeutic purposes. It is also known by a variety of other names including scriptotherapy (Riordan 1996) and life writing (Glover 2001). Writers such as Adams (1996a, b) and Schiwy (1996) use the terms 'journal' and 'diary' interchangeably, although as Adams (1996a, p. 32) writes, "... journals are often considered to be more interior and self-reflective than diaries". She explains journal therapy as "... the purposeful and intentional use of process writing to further psychological healing" (Ibid) and 'process writing' being "... characterised by fluidity of thought, leading to spontaneous and organic insights... as material from the unconscious mind ... is revealed and brought to conscious awareness" (Adams 1996b, p. 3).

Adams (1999) maintains that most people can use and respond to journal therapy. As with any therapeutic intervention, the activities, structure and pace must match the individual needs and abilities of each person. Adams (1999)

D. Western, *Gender-based Violence and Depression in Women*,
SpringerBriefs in Social Work, DOI: 10.1007/978-1-4614-7532-3_7,
© The Author(s) 2013

divides journaling activities into different categories depending on factors such as the degree of containment offered by an activity, how abstract or structured and concrete it is and how much intuitive knowledge might be needed. Activities that are "...well structured, concrete, practical and immediately useful ... (are) good when you're feeling overwhelmed, want information quickly, or don't have much time" (Adams 1999, p. 4).

Women and Journals

The women co-researchers in my research gave eloquent explanations of what journaling meant to them and why it was important. Phoebe commented: "(My journaling is) about me, my life, joys, pain, suffering and excitement. It entwines and unwinds the complexity of my life. It is self-talk—writing your own narrative. It is multilayered for me, like circles overlapping. It is about me and how I feel about it all; the effects it has on my highs and lows in life". Samantha explained that "(I'm not) wasting my time (when I journal) because I'm sitting and I'm thinking about it and doing it and I'm focused on it". Naomi journaled: "I probably only write in the journal, getting my thoughts onto a page. I'm in print here. Ooh, maybe it's an egotistical thing. Well it could be. I want my life to be documented as it is my life and no-one else knows how it is. Shit, I don't even know how it is at times. Well that last statement tells me it's not primarily an egotistical thing. It's therapeutic. It allows me to explore more of myself away from anything getting in the way".

Schiwy (1996) asserts that journaling, as a method of self-review, self-development and creativity, became more visible and attractive to women during the 1970s. Much development was occurring in the use of journaling as a therapeutic intervention, either in conjunction with therapists or for women on their own. This decade also witnessed the further development of feminism, the women's rights movement and consciousness-raising groups which all encouraged women to become more assertive, argue for equal rights, learn about themselves and where they belonged in society and explore and express their individuality and sense of identity. Moreover, issues such as sexual assault and domestic violence were named and identified and many women, who had experienced such traumas silently, were now more able to disclose them and receive counselling and support. Keeping a journal was an important part of this process for many women (Heilbrun 1988).

According to Schiwy (1996, p. 16) "...women have kept diaries in order to communicate with themselves, to explore the meaning of their lives, and to give form to their creative impulses". Rainer (1978, p. 18) states that a journal

> ... enables you to express feelings without inhibition, recognise and alter self-defeating habits of mind, and come to know and accept that self which is you. It is a sanctuary where all the disparate elements of a life—feelings, thoughts, dreams, hopes, fears, fantasies, practicalities, worries, facts, and intuitions—can merge to give you a sense of wholeness and coherence.

Peterson and Jones (2001, p. 59) believe that "…journals provide women with a space in which to record life stories and critical events, to solve problems, and to engage in personal discovery and self-awareness". Glover (2001, para 38), in fact, considered journals and life writing to be so powerful and full of possibilities that they

> … may mirror societal expectations of the writer or (they) may actively subvert such expectations. It may be based on the individual's perspective of real life, or written as the construction of the self as the writer would like to be or imagines she can be, her self constructed against the expectations of community.

We are starting to see, here, that journals and the process of journaling, have the potential to be powerful tools in assisting women to regain their self-confidence, sense of identity/subjectivity and capacity to think towards the future. The concepts of consciousness-raising and resistance, discussed in Chap. 6, can act as methods of repudiating gender-based violence against women and subsequent depression and regaining/reclaiming women's rights. Consciousness-raising and resistance can be cultivated within the journal—and perhaps even more powerfully within feminist group work through women's journaling groups.

Journaling is a highly individualised activity that is constructed and refined by each woman to suit her purposes, her motivation, her needs, her circumstances and her level of emotional comfort. Journaling consists of more than the content of the journal entries; journaling is a process. This reflects one of the characteristics of the recovery process described in Chap. 5; recovery from depression is a continuously evolving and dynamic process where what is learned and done during the process is often as important as the outcome.

Research into Journaling as a Therapeutic Intervention

Other than the research that I have undertaken, there is limited research in relation to journaling as a therapeutic intervention, particularly when exploring the areas of women, depression, journaling and group work together. Most of the research with some relevance to journaling concerns the activities of expressive writing, therapeutic writing and positive writing and their use in mediating the effects of traumatic or stressful experiences. Improvements in physical and mental health are common when people write about a traumatic event, and importantly, the thoughts and feelings that accompany this event (Baikie et al. 2012; Furnes and Dysvik 2012; Smyth and Pennebaker 1999, p. 74). In a meta-analysis of writing therapy research, van Emmerik et al. (2013) found that writing therapy resulted in reduced levels of post-traumatic stress and depressive symptoms, particularly for people with mild to moderate depression. Riordan (1996) highlights the importance of explaining experience through words "… verbally labelling and describing a trauma through writing allows an individual to cognitively process the event and gain a sense of control, thus reducing the work of inhibition" (Riordan 1996, p. 264).

The Use of Narratives in Journaling and Therapeutic Writing

I use the term 'narrative' to describe the themes and stories that women develop and use in their journals, not in relation to narrative therapy. We typically tell narratives and stories to communicate with others and to help us order, interpret and understand the events that happen to us and the ways in which we—and others—respond to these events (Czarniawska 2004). We often construct narratives when unexpected, unwanted or distressing events occur in our lives; when the happenings are outside our usual expectations. Developing narratives through journaling and therapeutic writing is a powerful way for women to organise events, make some meaning out of them, integrate thoughts and feelings and then be able to reach some level of understanding about their experiences. Narratives may be descriptive, exploratory or, when thinking about the future, imaginative (Polkinghorne 1988; Riessman 1993), all of which would enable expression, reflection, insight and comprehension for women undertaking therapeutic journaling activities. The process of constructing a narrative, as well as the narrative itself, is important in recovery from trauma. Stories may need to be reviewed and reconstructed as new information or different perspectives are achieved over time (Pennebaker and Seagal 1999). We can see here, once again, the importance of process as well as outcome, an important concept in feminist practice.

Wright (2009) observes that personal narratives have therapeutic potential and Schreiber (1996, p. 473) describes the overall process and narrative involved in women's recovery from depression as one of (re)defining the self; of finding the answer to "Who am I?" Women's narratives identified in other research (although not located in women's journals), include the role of social expectations and the importance of continuing on as wife, mother or worker irrespective of women's own needs; the loss and subsequent search for self and identity; and the presence and impact of violent, damaging or unsupportive relationships (Crowe 2002; Hurst 1999; Schreiber 1996; Stoppard and Scattolon 1999[1]). Recovery narratives identified by Fullagar and O'Brien (2012) include the immobilising effect of depression; recovery as a battle to control depression; and recovery as a journey of self-knowledge. Leavitt and Pill (1995, p. 138) note that in the process of developing narratives, people "…develop, refine, and reconstruct their personal sense of self. …writing opens new possibilities for storying our lives differently, providing a powerful therapeutic opportunity".

In Chap. 5, the idea of self was identified as central in understanding the development and impact of depression in women and in women's recovery from depression. The ways in which the development of narratives can assist in the recovery, restoration, renewal and regeneration of women's selves and identities further underscores the significance of the concept of self. Because women's

---

[1] Although these references are now dated, this reflects the limited amount of research in this field. Nevertheless, the findings remain relevant.

personal journals provide a space and opportunity for constructing and testing these narratives of the self, various journaling activities within the women's journaling groups include a focus on women's senses of self and identity.

The concept of narratives provides a major foundation underpinning the framework of the women's journaling groups. Four major narratives about women's understandings and experiences of depression provide a structure for women's journaling groups and can provide direction for the development of journaling, reflection and discussion activities. These narratives are:

(1) Identification and expression of emotions
(2) Identity, sense of self and self-value
(3) Structural and social roles, relationships and expectations
(4) Transformative choices, opportunities and accomplishments

I look at these narratives in more detail in Chap. 8.

Journaling Techniques, Materials and Prompts

Women's journaling involves much more than the best known traditional form of prose writing. Journaling processes and techniques are personal to each woman; not something that one can be directed to do and not something that is done in a routine, 'check the box' fashion (Adams 1990; Western 2003). I look now at the various journaling techniques and activities that can be offered in women's journaling groups.

(1) Traditional prose journaling techniques

- Dot points and lists
  This technique enables ideas to be captured rapidly and requires less structure and energy than prose writing. When women are imagining future possibilities and developing plans, this technique enables them to generate and contemplate ideas quickly and simply. In compiling a list, the journaling prompt might be: 'Develop a list of your wishes or plans'; 'Make a list of what makes you feel sad/happy/angry'; 'Create a list of your four funniest memories'. Individual ideas on these lists can then be explored, or used as prompts, in further journaling. Providing a time limit for this journaling activity can give women a sense of a boundary so if they are struggling with ideas, they are not left feeling exposed or unsuccessful.
- Unsent letters
  These can be a very powerful form of journaling where women write all the words, thoughts and messages they would like another person to hear and know, but in order to ensure safety, do not send the letter. This technique was favoured by Susan who explained: "I just keep writing them until I get the grammar and everything right and what I want to say right and I could

use a whole book. You know, they're not really to be published for any reason, they're just, this is what I want to say and that's what I do".

- Sentence starters

  This technique provides a starting point or direction for journaling. The facilitator provides the beginning of a sentence and women complete it with whatever comes to mind; for example, 'Now is the time for me to …' or 'When I hear women laughing, I think …'. Sentence starters may prompt women to journal in ways they have not previously considered or to journal about ideas they have not yet contemplated. They also create a boundary for the journaling. Boundaries provide a sense of safety for women, particularly those new to journaling or women concerned that journaling might open up topics they do not wish to think about. Naomi enjoyed using sentence starters because: "(They're) a really easy spot to start from if you're blocked or just to get you into somewhere else".

(2) Visual journaling techniques

Visual journaling techniques are helpful because women can, literally, see and view their thoughts, feelings, ideas, experiences, understandings and the connections between them. This journaling can assist women to see their situations and responses from different viewpoints. Jessica explained it this way, "Just seeing the visual images would tee up a whole lot of other things in my brain". "Positioning (in the collage) is very important. The visual stuff lets you do that I think. Lets you see where you're putting things in relation to yourself or whatever".

- Collage

  Collage, where women select pictures, words, phrases and other media that represent their experiences, feelings or perceptions, is a powerful journaling technique because it enables deep self expression and awareness, and is very effective in providing insights and ideas that women may not have achieved with other journaling techniques. The process of collage can be extended and added to when women write or draw about the images they have chosen because they then have an opportunity to explore the themes or ideas that evolve from the collage. This 'second layer' of journaling enables a deeper level of exploration and analysis of situations, questions, responses and thoughts to occur. Even the act of looking through magazines with a particular question in mind, selecting pictures and words, cutting them out, and keeping them securely can be considered, if not journaling itself, certainly a pre-cursor to it. This part of the process can be therapeutic as women become immersed in the process of thinking about themselves and their interactions, their thoughts, feelings, ideas and plans. Women may not always be able to explain why a particular image or word is evocative, but through further reflection with journaling or discussion with group members, this often becomes apparent and provides important insight.

  Collage does require more organising and access to materials so it may not suit or be possible for everyone.

- Painting and drawing

  Samantha viewed her paintings as a form of journaling because she expressed herself and her moods through them. She noted that painting did not usually just 'happen' for her; the whole process of thinking, planning, expressing and painting was considered and therapeutic. Abstract or literal drawings can facilitate extra depth and reflection for women. As Phoebe described, "I had some pictures about circles and in the circle, I had an oblong and I've gone, oh well, an oblong got in there; just goes to show maybe it's not as I see it. So that created another thought process".

- Mind mapping clusters

  These are similar to word association and are represented diagrammatically. They can be created in response to an emotion, event or question and be produced quite quickly, allowing for less conscious ideas to surface. As with the other visual journaling techniques, once a cluster or mind map is complete, further journaling can reveal unconscious connections and meanings and enable thoughts and feelings to be explored, analysed, made sense of and looked at in more depth. Creating clusters is a popular activity because it provides women with a lot of information about thoughts, feelings and events and because it is relatively easy and straightforward.

(3) Narrative journaling techniques

- Poems and stories

  This simply involves the creation of poetry and stories about one's experiences. Women often find that their accounts of their depression are present in their stories; not necessarily because they plan to include depression, but because the depression (feelings, thoughts and experiences), surfaces through the process of the journaling and because it is an integral part of women's lives.

- Dialogue

  This journaling technique assists women to think about different perspectives and understandings. An imagined dialogue can construct communication with other people, events, situations, parts of the body, the perspective of another person or anything else that a woman has a question about. It can be used in order to achieve some insight into relationships or events. The rationale is that each woman has her own knowledge and ideas about how to respond to, and begin to change, problematic situations. An example of a dialogue-based journaling activity might invite women to 'Dialogue between the depressed part of you and the less depressed part of you' or 'Dialogue between the present and the future; how might what I'm doing now change what my situation will be like in 4 weeks?' Susan enjoyed the following activity using dialogue, "Talking to yourself as a ninety year old saying to yourself 'If I did this action, what would happen?' And the ninety year old says 'Well, I don't remember that happening really, why is it such a big issue?' So you actually are challenging yourself with wisdom".

- Stream of consciousness writing
  The aim of stream of consciousness writing is to write with nothing in particular in mind, but as quickly as possible without stopping and without thinking about, or editing, what is being written and to do this for a defined amount of time. This technique aims to access deeper, less concrete thoughts than might normally be achieved by formal, structured and edited writing. My experience with this technique is that: "You don't really make sentences because you just keep writing and because you're thinking as fast as you can, writing as fast as you can, you don't actually come to use a sentence....you try to tap into, you know, a really sort of deep subconscious part of the mind. While you're writing it, you're thinking this will make absolutely no sense at all. But when you stop and you read over it, it does. It seems weird, but you can understand it".
- Performance journaling
  This is a non-traditional form of journaling which may include singing (singing a song from a musical for instance), and playing characters from books or films. Similar, in some ways, to psychodrama, I term this journaling, 'performance journaling' because it has the characteristics of acting and performing, albeit for oneself and not an audience. Phoebe engaged in performance journaling and this typically involved playing a character from a book or a film and performing a text; "a chapter" as she called it: "Like if I get on the horse and ride I can play a character in a book and take a couple of the dogs and they can be part of that character in the book, I can do some really good stuff in a thirty minute ride!"

Performance journaling is generally undertaken because it is experienced as a safer way to express oneself, particularly when a woman lacks confidence in her writing, spelling and grammatical skills. Phoebe explained it this way, "I do that (performance journaling), not to be creative, because I don't like putting pen to paper and the punctuation. I could journal. I couldn't care less whether I have a capital letter or anything else, so that's my way of doing it; in a safe space without being criticised because the pen on paper isn't making as good as what it should be".

Women's Use of Multiple and New Journaling Techniques

Using more than one technique to journal about the same topic or theme can bring out different responses, different perspectives and different levels of insight into a situation. In order to achieve the most comprehensive advantages of journaling and the most thorough understandings of themselves and of their depression, women would benefit from using a variety of journaling techniques, including techniques they have not previously tried. New journaling techniques can lead to new ideas, information, insights and awarenesses, even if these are, at times, confronting. Adair commented that "I have done a lot of different types of journaling, so to do something that's active and, a scary word for me, creative, would be good to do".

Here are two examples of how women described their varied ways of journaling: Barbra viewed her journaling on a continuum. She tended to use more traditional forms of prose writing at each end of the continuum; these being times when she was experiencing strong emotions, either positive or negative, that were overwhelming her and she felt a need to "Write it down, work it out!" In the middle of the continuum, she placed the journaling that comprised collage and collected items such as sayings, articles and thoughts from various sources that she often used as prompts for journaling. "Quite frankly I get really bored with writing but I'll collect poems or I'll collect sayings and something I've found in the newspaper or a picture or a cartoon or something and they're all collected and put into scrap books". Susan realised that the form of her journaling changed across time and that: "I actually journal in a heap of different ways". She incorporated photographs into her journal, for instance, and had photographed a sequence of shots to show emotional change in someone or in her own emotional response.

Journaling Materials

Encouraging women to experiment with the style, format and presentation of the journal can open up new possibilities for the ways in which women journal and express themselves. For example, the use of colour in journaling (through different colour pens, pencils, paints, paper), can add creativity and flexibility to the journaling process. As Jessica remembered, "Having colour really changed what I did and how I recorded things. I was kind of using bold headings and different kinds of writing and not because I'm trained, just because I love painting and colour. And it's really about going, okay, what's the feeling, what colour do I need to express that? What shape is it? And just kind of letting it happen and I really enjoy that, yeah". Consideration can be given to the journal itself too; is it lined or unlined, hard or soft cover, glued together or spiral bound? For some women who have experienced violence and depression, the simple act of choosing a journal, something that is theirs, can be deeply pleasing. This can be part of the therapeutic process too.

Conclusion

Journals provide a personal space for women to express their thoughts and feelings, reach understandings about their situations and develop and test out narratives about their selves and their identities. Narratives are vital components of journaling and underpin the activities integrated into the women's journaling groups. Journaling can be undertaken in a variety of ways and with different materials depending on each woman's preference, needs and setting. The process of journaling can be as important and transformative as the outcomes of the journaling.

References

Adams K (1990) Journal to the self. Warner Books Inc., New York

Adams K (1996a) Journal writing as a powerful adjunct to therapy. J Poet Ther 10(1):31–37

Adams K (1996b) The structured journal therapy assessment: a report on 50 cases. J Poet Ther 10(2):77–85

Adams K (1999) Writing as therapy. Couns Hum Dev 31(5):1–16

Baikie K, Geerligs L, Wilhelm K (2012) Expressive writing and positive writing for participants with mood disorders: an online randomized controlled trial. J Affect Disord 136:310–319

Crowe M (2002) Reflexivity and detachment: a discursive approach to women's depression. Nurs Inq 9(2):126–132

Czarniawska B (2004) Narratives in social science research. Sage, London

Fullagar S, O'Brien W (2012) Immobility, battles, and the journey of feeling alive: women's metaphors of self-transformation through depression and recovery. Qual Health Res 22(8):1063–1072

Furnes B, Dysvik E (2012) Therapeutic writing and chronic pain: experiences of therapeutic writing in a cognitive behavioural programme for people with chronic pain. J Clin Nurs 21:3372–3381

Glover B (2001) Women's life writing. Int Aust Stud Assoc 6(3):1–6

Heilbrun C (1988) Writing a woman's life. Ballantine Books, New York

Hurst S (1999) Legacy of betrayal: a grounded theory of becoming demoralised from the perspective of women who have been depressed. Can Psychol 40(2):179

Leavitt R, Pill C (1995) Composing a self through writing: the ego and the ink. Smith Coll Stud Soc Work 65(2):137–149

Pennebaker J, Seagal J (1999) Forming a story: the health benefits of narrative. J Clin Psychol 55(10):1243–1254

Peterson E, Jones A (2001) Women, journal writing, and the reflective process. New Dir Adult Contin Educ 90:59–67

Polkinghorne D (1988) Narrative knowing and the human sciences. State University of New York Press, Albany

Rainer T (1978) The new diary. Jeremy P. Tarcher/Putnam, New York

Riessman C (1993) Narrative analysis. Sage Publications, London

Riordan R (1996) Scriptotherapy: therapeutic writing as a counselling adjunct. J Couns Dev 74(3):263–270

Schiwy M (1996) A voice of her own: women and the journal-writing journey. Fireside, New York

Schreiber R (1996) (Re)Defining my self: women's process of recovery from depression. Qual Health Res 6(4):469–491

Smyth J, Pennebaker J (1999) Sharing one's story: translating emotional experiences into words as a coping tool. In: Snyder C (ed) Coping: the psychology of what works. Oxford University Press, Oxford, pp 70–90

Stoppard J, Scattolon Y (1999) Getting on with life: women's experiences and ways of coping with depression. Can Psychol 40(2):205

van Emmerik A, Reijntjes A, Kamphuis J (2013) Writing therapy for posttraumatic stress: a meta-analysis. Psychother Psychosom 82:82–88

Western D (2003) Inside out: a journaling kit. Innovative Resources, Bendigo

Wright J (2009) Autoethnography and therapy writing on the move. Qual Inq 15(4):623–640

Chapter 8
The Women's Journaling Group Program Model

Abstract This chapter provides an overview of the Women's Journaling Group Program model. Building on discussions in previous chapters about concepts such as the self, identity, narratives, women's experiences of depression and journaling styles and techniques, I introduce the three major components of the model; frameworks, narratives and threads. Journaling is presented as a process and as a form of action and engagement. I further explore how journaling and feminist group work can activate the methods of consciousness-raising and resistance (as introduced in Chap. 6) and encourage women in their recovery and transitions away from violence and depression.

Keywords Journaling · Women · Action · Consciousness-raising · Resistance · Narrative · Self · Depression · Recovery · Feminist group work · Gender-based violence

The Underpinning Principles of the Women's Journaling Group Program Model

Journaling as a Process and as a Form of Action

Journaling is a process and the 'doing' of journaling and the manner in which it is undertaken, is as important as the outcome. As Naomi commented, "I see it as a process, it's like I'm getting my ideas out and processing it in a better way than I could just in my head". As seen in Chap. 7, the process of journaling can involve choosing the journaling techniques, activities, materials, contexts and times for journaling. Women learn about themselves, their situations, what they need to be different and how they might reach a different place and space through the processes of journaling. This occurs through undertaking journaling activities and through participating in a journaling group with other women. Women build narratives about violence and depression in their journals. Their journaling is not a passive or random activity and the ways in which narratives are constructed enable women to understand the place and meaning of violence and depression in their lives. Whilst the entries in women's journals are not necessarily constructed to form an orderly or sequential narrative, individual extracts constitute examples of experiences from the women's lives. Taken together, larger narratives emerge and unfold.

The Women's Journaling Group Program Model

The model consists of:

- *Two frameworks.* The frameworks head the model and each framework describes women's responses to depression and their subsequent modes of journaling.
- *Four major narratives.* I first introduced the concept of narratives in Chap. 7. Each narrative can be found in both frameworks.
- *Nineteen threads.* These are very specific threads that come from the four narratives. They describe the themes within each narrative and the themes and content that may be seen in women's journaling.

I now consider these components in more detail and show how they interconnect with each other and how they inform the development of journaling activities within women's journaling groups.

The Two Overarching Frameworks

Women's responses to depression and their subsequent methods of journaling fall into two frameworks. One framework is the **Considered Acknowledgement, Acceptance and Contemplation Framework** (Diagram 8.1). The other framework is the **Proactive Resistance, Rehearsal, Agency and Action Framework**. Each Framework reflects particular ways that women have of responding to, understanding and managing their depression and the surrounding influences, events and contexts. Women's thoughts about their depression and the degree of agency, or control, they perceive they hold in achieving some change in their depression and in the ways they live their lives are also represented in the frameworks.

When women respond to depression with Considered Acknowledgement, Acceptance and Contemplation, they identify, express and explore their depressed feelings and thoughts. This Framework is characterised by emotion, experiencing the emotions surrounding depression and, at times, staying with the pain, confusion

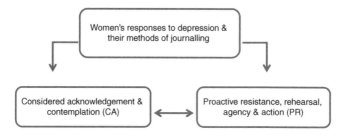

Diagram 8.1   The two frameworks: Women's responses to depression and their subsequent methods of journaling

and numbness that often typify depression. This is a time where women realise and accept that they are experiencing some form of depression, sometimes not for the first time. Women then recognise the imperative to take some time to settle and get to a point where they can start to make some decisions about how they want to manage their situation. Through their responses to depression and through journaling, women are engaging in a form of action because, by identifying their depression and factors that seem to be contributing to (or reducing) it, they begin to think about how to manage it.

When women respond to depression with Proactive Resistance, Rehearsal, Agency and Action, their journaling, thinking and behaviour is more positive, resolute, concrete and forward-looking. This assists women to take stronger overt, engaged and communicative action to further understand, manage and lessen their depression. The impetus for women to take this different form of action is often a realisation of how 'fed-up' they are with their situation and feelings of anger are frequently experienced at this point. While the anger needs to be used and expressed appropriately and safely, it does provide energy and motivation for women to take proactive action to change their situations and to reclaim their rights. The activities and concepts of consciousness-raising and resistance become important at this time because they contribute to women understanding they have rights to be safe, make decisions and be assertive. Thus, the journal is a venue in which women rehearse and facilitate changes in their lives and integrate their experiences of violence and depression into their identities.

The two frameworks are not mutually exclusive and do not represent chronological stages where women need to complete the activities and tasks within one framework before proceeding on to the second framework. Paralleling the multi-directional nature of experiencing and recovering from depression, women's journaling is characterised by its cyclical, recursive nature and recurring, interacting patterns. Journaling is an ongoing process of expression, awareness, consciousness-raising, learning, resisting, rehearsing, experimenting, reflecting, contemplating, resisting and rehearsing again, experimenting again and immersing oneself in the process again.

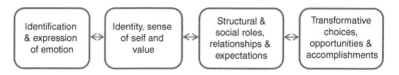

Diagram 8.2   The four narratives within the Women's Journaling Group Program model

The Four Narratives Within the Frameworks

The four narratives, which often overlap with each other, are found within the Considered Acknowledgement, Acceptance and Contemplation Framework and within the Proactive Resistance, Rehearsal, Agency and Action Framework. The narratives are:

1. Identification and expression of emotions
2. Identity, sense of self and self-value
3. Structural and social roles, relationships and expectations
4. Transformative choices, opportunities and accomplishments

   Diagram 8.2 shows the four narratives.

The Threads Within the Narratives

Each narrative is made up of one or more 'threads'. Some threads are more likely to be found in the Considered Acknowledgement, Acceptance and Contemplation Framework (Table 5.1) and others in the Proactive Resistance, Rehearsal, Agency and Action Framework (Table 5.2) whilst some threads are found in both Frameworks. The threads and the narratives provide practitioners with ideas and directions about the themes and content that are generally useful for women to journal about and to reflect on as they participate in women's journaling groups.

   Tables 8.1 and 8.2 show the threads that are located in each of the Frameworks of the Women's Journaling Group Program model.

   When all these components—the frameworks, the narratives and the threads—are put together, we can see how they interact and build on each other to form the model. Diagram 8.3 shows the full Women's Journaling Group Program model with the frameworks, narratives, threads and the relationships between them.

How Might the Women's Journaling Group Program Model?

The frameworks, narratives and threads provide direction and inspiration for the development of journaling activities and creation of areas of discussion and reflection for facilitators of women's journaling groups. They also provide one

Table 8.1 The threads within the Considered Acknowledgement, Acceptance and Contemplation Framework

1. The emergence of women's voices; the expression of emotion
2. Understanding the fluctuation and unpredictability of depression
3. Expression and change: depression and anger as motivators
4. Reconnection with the self and reestablishment of identity; conflict between inner and outer worlds
5. Consciousness-raising
6. Consciousness-raising and resistance: medicalisation and labelling of depression
7. Understanding social change and loss
8. Assessing and re-assessing connections with other people
9. Crucial movement and a sense of change
10. New insights, understandings, connections and transformations
11. Rehearsal: opportunities for planning, considering alternatives, making choices

Table 8.2 The threads within the Proactive Resistance, Rehearsal, Agency and Action Framework

1. Identification and expression of enlivening feelings and affirmative experiences
2. The transformed and stronger sense of identity, self and self-value
3. Resistance and transformative action
4. Rehearsal: interpersonal relationships
5. Resistance: change and transformation
6. Imagination, creativity and consideration of a hopeful future
7. Rehearsal
8. Reflection and change

particular way of identifying where women may be in terms of their understanding of their depression and their thoughts about how they would like to respond to not only the experiences of depression, but to the contributing factors, impacts and, of course, the violence they have also experienced. Not all threads will be relevant for every woman's journaling group so practitioners will need to assess what topics seem meaningful and engage women in the selection of topic areas.

To look in further depth at the way in which the model can work, I will now explore the ways in which the narratives and threads are situated in the Considered Acknowledgement, Acceptance and Contemplation Framework. I will then look at the four narratives and associated threads within the Proactive Resistance, Rehearsal, Agency and Action Framework. Further discussion about practice knowledge, skills and implications is undertaken in Chap. 10.

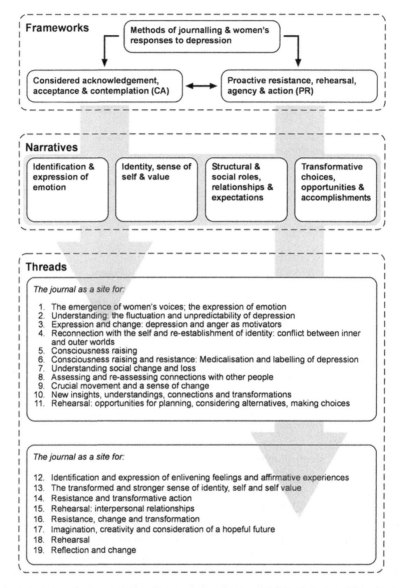

Frameworks

Methods of journalling & women's responses to depression

Considered acknowledgement, acceptance & contemplation (CA) ⟷ Proactive resistance, rehearsal, agency & action (PR)

Narratives

Identification & expression of emotion

Identity, sense of self & value

Structural & social roles, relationships & expectations

Transformative choices, opportunities & accomplishments

Threads

The journal as a site for:

1. The emergence of women's voices; the expression of emotion
2. Understanding: the fluctuation and unpredictability of depression
3. Expression and change: depression and anger as motivators
4. Reconnection with the self and re-establishment of identity: conflict between inner and outer worlds
5. Consciousness raising
6. Consciousness raising and resistance: Medicalisation and labelling of depression
7. Understanding social change and loss
8. Assessing and re-assessing connections with other people
9. Crucial movement and a sense of change
10. New insights, understandings, connections and transformations
11. Rehearsal: opportunities for planning, considering alternatives, making choices

The journal as a site for:

12. Identification and expression of enlivening feelings and affirmative experiences
13. The transformed and stronger sense of identity, self and self value
14. Resistance and transformative action
15. Rehearsal: interpersonal relationships
16. Resistance, change and transformation
17. Imagination, creativity and consideration of a hopeful future
18. Rehearsal
19. Reflection and change

Diagram 8.3   The Women's Journaling Group Program model with the frameworks, narratives, threads

Incorporating the Women's Journaling Group Model into Practice

Framework 1:	Considered Acknowledgement, Acceptance and Contemplation
Narrative 1:	Identification and expression of emotions
Thread 1:	The emergence of women's voices: the expression of emotion

Including opportunities to identify and express emotion and feelings in journaling activities is crucial. Typical emotions surrounding depression are frustration, anger, embarrassment, loss, grief, sadness and hurt. Some lessening in the severity of women's depression can occur when feelings and emotions are identified and expressed through journaling. This enables women to slowly start to consider the possibilities of movement within their depression. Adair described it this way: "If for me, when I'm in the feeling, lots of feelings, and I start to, it's almost like spill the feelings, that gives opportunity for the rest of me to sort of actually get in line and then have a say and then sort of pull it together. And that's finding a voice too, that's finding my voice and not just the impact of everything else that's going on". Barbra reflected that I'm feeling flat and shitful, depressed or whatever but I'll go and explore that a bit and yeah, there's something going on. And so the journaling can kind of help to unearth that a bit. It might not necessarily mean that I'll do anything about it, but at least I know where it came from". Adella was clear about the importance of emotion: "When depressed, I'm fully aware of all my feelings. I'm dealing with stuff, I'm right there, feeling the pain". "Being me includes the me when I'm depressed. Have to be in the depression and acknowledge it".

Framework 1:	Considered acknowledgement, acceptance and contemplation
Narrative 1:	Identification and expression of emotions
Thread 2:	Understanding the fluctuation and unpredictability of depression

The emergence and continuation of depression is often unpredictable and it can fluctuate over time in its nature and degree. This perceived arbitrary nature of depression underscores the importance of the women's journals as sites for the expression of emotions and women's attempts to understand their depression. As Kate journaled, "Here I am writing again to hopefully appease my misery. I feel as though I am beating my head up against a brick wall. I try so very hard and feel ok. Then suddenly I feel totally lost and hopeless. I feel it is all too hard". Whilst this fluctuation and unpredictability is frustrating and confusing, it can provide a small sign to women who journal about it that change can occur and that their depression can lift.

Framework 1:	Considered acknowledgement, acceptance and contemplation
Narrative 1:	Identification and expression of emotions
Thread 3:	Expression and change: depression and anger as motivators

Many women prefer to journal than to communicate verbally when they are depressed. However, this does not hold true for all women and some women are not ready to journal until they start to feel angry. As practitioners, this is important knowledge to have so we can monitor women's readiness to journal, to shape activities appropriately and contain and hold any complex and overwhelming emotions for women that may emerge through journaling. Journaling can provide women with a safe place to help them stop the running commentary in their heads; the conversation that goes nowhere, but keeps repeating and reinforcing the depressed feelings, the concerns, the self-consciousness, the guilt and the doubts. Adair journaled about her depression and anger: "The stable point of my depression is my anger. It's all about me, me, me. Spiralling inward and down-ward. My madness. And that's certainly not an acceptable way to behave. To be angry and out there. So putting it on paper and daring to explore that". Naomi journaled: "No one could understand how I was feeling, cause I didn't know. And it's taken me a while to even realise I was feeling anything. In a nutshell I'm pissed off". Jessica explained the importance of having a journal as a safe place to express anger: "A really good way for me in my anger (is) to vent my feelings so that I can understand them and probably, I don't let go of the anger, it takes a bit longer than that, but at least often, it gives me a way to plan what I might do when I've settled". Rachael journaled about a positive side of anger: "(The energy from anger can) prove people wrong".

Framework 1:	Considered acknowledgement, acceptance and contemplation
Narrative 2:	Identity, sense of self and self-value
Thread 4:	Reconnection with the self and reestablishment of identity: conflict between inner and outer worlds

Repeated experiences of feeling unsure about their own identity and feeling unrecognised and unnoticed by other people can contribute to a reduced sense of self and self-value for women. The loss of a positive connection with the self is problematic. This can occur, for example, when women feel they are constantly meeting the unrelenting and overwhelming demands of other people, receiving very little in return, and when restricted opportunities to talk about what they are thinking or how they are feeling result in women feeling unable to act as the person they would like to be. Zelda journaled, "I don't actually recognize myself. I'm so aware of what's going on for everybody else, I don't have any solidity as to who I am". Barbra described her thoughts: "There are times where you're just so much in automatic that you know, the core stuff is just hidden away there, under those layers and layers and all this crap and dump stuff, and I think it's really hard to get at and maybe that's just part of life at that stage". Journaling provides women with opportunities to develop, strengthen and test out their 'voice'. Naomi's journaling shows a strong example of this: "This is no longer about me. I've drawn the line and he's crossed it again. I can't keep punishing myself. There is (sic) no more lines to cross without compromising more of myself. Knowing this will keep me strong, focused and resilient". Penny realised, "Because if I'm not heard, I lose sight of who I am, what I think, or I lose touch with my feelings. It makes it more difficult to express them and then I feel out of control and not in touch with myself. Gets too difficult to express myself, so I go into myself and other people's needs are more important".

Framework 1:	Considered acknowledgement, acceptance and contemplation
Narrative 3:	Structural and social roles, relationships and expectations
Thread 5:	Consciousness-raising

The likelihood of women developing and experiencing depression increases as the discrepancy between women's identity, sense of self and their own needs on the one hand, and social assumptions and expectations, the social roles in which they engage and the self they present to the world on the other, increases. A figurative mask, in effect, may be used by women to cover up their real selves, desires and needs in order to conform to the expectations of other people and/or of 'society's' idea of how and who they should be. The outside mask enables women to be seen as 'coping', but this reinforces for the women that they do not have a voice or strong sense of self/identity. Through journaling, women's consciousness, awareness and questions about these contributing factors to depression can be raised. Jessica's journaling read: "Because they're things I can not seem to change. You know? They're things I can not seem to have any dent on and so they're immovable and when I hit up against them, they're not going to change and it's my having to regroup around that". Kate also journaled about these issues: "You might smile, you might laugh, but all the time there is a shadow that clouds the light from your life. There is a grey coldness that is yours for the rest of your days and for a person to have to live with that is sheer hell. I might look ok but believe me, I am not ok at all!!" Adella journaled that "People expect me to conform then I feel really frustrated, angry, a sense of sadness about not being my real self. Sad that people can not appreciate someone being different or seeing something from a different point of view". Zoe reflected that "People expect me to be agreeable, easy going and not have strong opinions about things. Then I feel that I don't matter, I'm not valued, and angry with myself for not standing up for myself and allowing myself to be used".

Framework 1:	Considered acknowledgement, acceptance and contemplation
Narrative 3:	Structural and social roles, relationships and expectations
Thread 6:	Consciousness-raising: medicalisation and labelling of depression

This is a specific area where women's consciousness can be shared and raised. It may not be relevant for all groups to journal about. Women have different views about the necessity for and desirability of medication for depression. When women have an understanding that depression can be a response to limited choices and limited flexibility in their lives, the medicalisation of depression does not always sit well with them. As Barbra noted, "If we know that other people have similar problems, it's like, oh, well maybe it's not just me. What else is going on here that maybe is contributing to all of that?"

Framework 1:	Considered acknowledgement, acceptance and contemplation
Narrative 3:	Structural and social roles, relationships and expectations
Thread 7:	Understanding social change and loss

Feeling uncertain, insecure, unanchored and confused, particularly in response to situations that may be beyond their ability to influence and manage, is common for women experiencing violence and depression. The damaging impact of these feelings on the women's sense of self and capacity to look forward is considerable. Jessica's uncertainty is evident: "I feel a bit purposeless at present. A bit at sea and lost. ... I guess I just don't really know what to do with myself and my life. Where to head—how to focus. So confused". In sorrow, Kate journaled, "Sometimes I wonder what I have done to receive so much pain and misery". As practitioners we need to watch for women erroneously taking responsibility for events that are outside their doing or their control whilst not placing them in the role of 'victim'. Recognising the many different forms of loss and the grief that can accompany these losses is vital for women and practitioners have a role to play here.

Framework 1:	Considered acknowledgment, acceptance and contemplation
Narrative 3:	Structural and social roles, relationships and expectations
Thread 8:	Assessing and re-assessing connections with other people

Interpersonal relationships with partners, family members and work colleagues play a vital role in providing connections and linking women with community. When these relationships are stable, safe and generous, women experience support and strength in their recovery processes. However, fragile and perplexing interpersonal relationships are typically characterised by high involvement and investment of emotion and little alteration in the patterns of interaction or problems encountered. As Zelda journaled, "Family relationships are difficult because I don't say what I think. I don't speak my mind. Takes so much resolve to have a different voice. I feel like the underlying thing isn't touched. My world and my reality seem so different from that of some others". Magdalena reflected, "People expect me to be available when they need me and go away when they don't. I don't get recognition. It would be nice for them to know that I'm there and include me in their lives. For myself". Naomi journaled, "I wasn't considered in your actions—there was no respect. But it hadn't occurred to me that it would be lack of respect cause it's one word I remember you explaining the importance of". Kate journaled her experience: "I feel really let down. One minute they profess undying love and affection – the next – or the rest of the time- I am a forgotten burden".

Framework 1:	Considered acknowledgment, acceptance and contemplation
Narrative 4:	Transformative choices, opportunities and accomplishments
Thread 9:	Crucial movement and a sense of change

When journaling, there is a difference between rumination and being stuck on one topic or in the same place, and journaling in depth about a topic, particularly when women attempt to untangle their thinking and to understand meanings, processes and links. Naomi's experience is "I notice when I do journal that I start off on a point and by the time I feel like that's enough writing, I'm at the same point. It's not that I've gone round and round in circles and I haven't moved on. It's like where I started, is then filled in with all the explanation. And it's 'oh, okay, that's why.' All the bits in the middle filled it up with the answers". Practitioners have a role in guiding women to notice changes they have made in their thinking, their perceptions and their ideas over time. Women can also do this for each other through discussions and reflections within journaling groups. Women's awareness of movement and change can motivate further journaling to explore how these changes might have been initiated, supported and sustained.

Framework 1:	Considered acknowledgment, acceptance and contemplation
Narrative 4:	Transformative choices, opportunities and accomplishments
Thread 10:	New insights, understandings, connections and transformations

Over time, journaling can provide insights and revelations for women. This may not always be a comfortable process and women may need to be supported through this. Phoebe noted, "I find it (journaling) as a rule, a pretty good reflection of, oh this is what's happening, this is what's attached to it, this is the thread, this is why that. Some insights you don't particularly like, but others are okay". Samantha developed confidence and certainty: "I'm not going back to the same thing (the depression)". Naomi realised that "Journalling allows you to recognise that and go 'oh I remember that, now I get it, and I'm still reacting to it.' Do I want to continue reacting to that in this way?"

Framework 1:	Considered acknowledgment, acceptance and contemplation
Narrative 4:	Transformative choices, opportunities and accomplishments
Thread 11:	Rehearsal: opportunities for planning, considering alternatives, making choices

After the expression and processing of information, ideas, thoughts and feelings in the journal, women often move to a different stage within their depression. When women make their depression concrete and real in the journal, they may then feel clearer and more confident to consider possible alternatives and choices. This is Jessica's experience: "So I don't necessarily then get my journal out and go, okay, time to work my way through the plan. But it's kind of like, being able to see that there's a possible path to follow allows me to feel less distressed. It gives me some ideas about some ways forward. I may only use one of them, but at least that's something new and it means I'm actually trying something else instead of just, oh, shit, you know, whatever". For Naomi, "Okay, it's there, it's obviously an issue, but it's for me and the next step is acting on it. How do I address this, I know I have to". Whilst change may be desired, it is not always easy as Zoe journaled, "Depression often becomes your identity; you're the depressed one in the family. It's really hard when you're getting better. How do you juggle that? If you've done that role, it's a difficult change for the system". Magdalena journaled similar dilemmas, "Will I stop being me? It's a real barrier. The person you are now has to die, so the other person can be born. Like rejection; you're not good enough. You've got to be something else".

Framework Two: Proactive Resistance, Rehearsal, Agency and Action

Whilst narratives in the Considered Acknowledgement, Acceptance and Contemplation Framework tend to be emotionally full, candid and painful, narratives within the Proactive Resistance, Rehearsal, Agency and Action Framework are more uplifting, encouraging, purposeful and forward-looking. Negative, blaming and judgemental narratives are more likely to be rebuffed. Narratives of identity, sense of self and self-value become clearer, more resilient and positively defined whilst the narratives around structural and social roles, relationships and expectations show greater clarity and expression of women's own needs, priorities and expectations.

Journaling now includes a stronger cognitive component. This more concrete, practical form of journaling may be used by women when they want to complete a task, solve problems, or make plans within the journal. Journaling in this Framework also includes room for imagination, creativity and anticipation. Narratives of transformative choices, opportunities and accomplishments are particularly important in this mode of journaling and indicate women's decision making processes, plans for action and lessening of depression.

Framework 2:	Proactive Resistance, Rehearsal, Agency and Action
Narrative 1:	Identification and expression of emotions
Thread 12:	Identification and expression of enlivening feelings and affirmative experiences

Journaling now includes the identification and expression of optimism and pleasure as shown by Adair, "And I smile at my optimism and general amusement that is my life. Fortunately I can smile warmly at this story with all these times, all the stories, fitting in". Closely linked to the journaling of hopeful, optimistic and confident emotions, is a shifting in the women's perceptions and ideas about themselves and the impact of their depression. This shift often begins when women focus on affirmative aspects of their lives. Kate journaled: "I do say thank you for some simpler things – like having friends think of me and giving me a call. Such little things but at the time I'm so grateful. Thank you for my health. Thank you God".

Framework 2:	Proactive Resistance, Rehearsal, Agency and Action
Narrative 2:	Identity, sense of self and self-value
Thread 13:	Transformed and stronger sense of identity, self and self-value

As women's depression lifts, their sense of self and self-value strengthens and enables them to make decisions about themselves and to take action that previously they would not have considered or completed. Adair journaled, "Entering into self-exploration has at times been exciting, and sometimes really difficult. During these times, my self that has been buried away often finds a voice in journaling". Jessica realised, "So you kind of clear off the layers of society and conditioning and then do the authentic bit, which is fantastic". Journals can provide women with an opportunity to identify what is important in their lives and what gives them a sense of stability, rootedness and meaning. By declaring their needs and priorities, women can begin the process of transformation by understanding and accepting they have a right to assertively ask for and expect certain qualities, factors or behaviours from people and situations around them. Women perceive new happenings and events as opportunities to explore their skills, interests and self-identity. Zoe journaled about her motivations and interests: "Nephews; spend a lot of time with them and this is where my creative stuff comes in. Playing games with them. You have to be in the moment with them. Dogs are good for that too. When I don't feel like my world is going ok, but I can be responsible for their care & safety even when I can't quite do that for myself". Penny also identified positives, "Painting, drawing, scribbling, cutting, pasting. Beach, nature, exploring, bike riding, walking, getting amongst it. Getting in touch with nature and my love for nature; that I'm part of nature and therefore my love for myself. Something that I've been working on to be a part of it and have that link".

Framework 2:	Proactive Resistance, Rehearsal, Agency and Action
Narrative 2:	Identity, sense of self and self-value
Thread 14:	Resistance and transformative action

As the women's sense of identity, self and self-value expands and strengthens, an awareness of their rights and capacity to be assertive often develops. Taking action, either within the journal or outside it, is a vital step in the progress toward recovering a sense of self and lessening depression. Taking action can result from resistance to the factors that contribute to depression. Whilst changes are exciting, the process is not necessarily easy or straightforward. Naomi journaled "Letting myself be deserving is one thing but now I need to expect it from others, and myself, and then keep that expectation at a 'deserving' level".

Framework 2:	Proactive Resistance, Rehearsal, Agency and Action
Narrative 3:	Structural and social roles, relationships and expectations
Thread 15:	Rehearsal: interpersonal relationships

Exploring relationships, particularly what they want from relationships and the ways in which they expect to be treated, is an important transformative activity for women recovering from depression and living with or leaving violent relationships. It is important to note that leaving a violent relationship can be a time of extremely high danger for women. If this planning is occurring within a women's journaling group, practitioners need to be aware of potential risks and ensure women are supported and linked in with appropriate resources and services. Susan journaled about her relationship with her sister, "But, I'm over her now. Had a big cry, right, stuff that, and I'm over it. I still love her and she's my sister, but she's there. And I'm here". Naomi realised that "The conversations were pointless, increasingly slurred and made me feel increasingly uncomfortable. I don't want to be exposed to this any more. What is it that makes this okay?" Jessica's rehearsal in her journal noted "(I will) speak more honestly and clearly. Air my views. Have some needs met; e.g. Feeling respected. Feel ok whilst with her".

Framework 2:	Proactive Resistance, Rehearsal, Agency and Action
Narrative 4:	Transformative choices, opportunities and accomplishments
Thread 16:	Resistance, change and transformation

Women may use their journals to resist and to seek and ask for support and guidance. Jessica journaled "Lord help me to create a life, help me to find friends. Help me to become whole again. Healed, healthy and fulfilled. Not bitter, angry and empty. Thank you". Resistance within women's journals can take the forms of envisioning difference, making and exercising choices. As Zoe journaled, "Journaling is part of that resistance. It's saying, I'm not going to do what I should. Giving to yourself at times". Naomi raised questions in her journal, "So what has to change? But what next? I want something that I can sink my teeth into, get excited about and be passionate about. So I will need to explore what that looks like". Adair realised that change required action: "If I choose to start journaling, then I know that I'm going to actually start facing the reality of what's going on for me. But I can't sit back and wallow if I journal because it's (now out there)".

Framework 2:	Proactive Resistance, Rehearsal, Agency and Action
Narrative 4:	Transformative choices, opportunities and accomplishments
Thread 17:	Imagination, creativity and consideration of a hopeful future

Imagination and creativity can assist women to strengthen their sense of self and self-value, to visualise how their situations might be different, and to consider how the factors that contribute to their depression might be lessened and resisted. Jessica journaled "Unlocking that other world, that world that maybe has potential and is separate to where you are right now, where it might be problem focused". Adair shared that "I began a scrap book without a theme in the beginning, focusing on my life, the future". Susan described the process as "Using the past to go forward". And Kate journaled her hopes: "I have another dream that one day I will find the 'perfect' man who will share my life and we will work together through everything. There! I've put it on paper!! And we will grow old together". Penny realised that "(I journal) when I need to get back in touch with myself. Remind myself of what's important to me; what my goals and achievements are and when I want to give to myself". The wishing, imagining or planning in the women's journals is important, not always for the nature of the wishes or plans, but for the women's capacity to think ahead and away from their current situation. Women are generally energised and inspired to undertake imaginative journaling when they are together in a journaling group.

Framework 2:	Proactive Resistance, Rehearsal, Agency and Action
Narrative 4:	Transformative choices, opportunities and accomplishments
Thread 18:	Rehearsal

Rehearsal is also an important activity in threads eleven and fifteen and the concerns are similar here. For some women, the time comes when they want to share their insights or plans within the journal with another person. This might be with the person about whom the journaling was undertaken or women may simply wish to check out their ideas. Although potentially confronting, conversations and challenges from other people can provide helpful feedback. As Naomi journaled, "You have to have conversations with other people so they know, oh, that's where she's coming from and that's her new position on things or whatever. You can't just go 'I'm here now and you're going to understand that'. You know, you have to then go and have that conversation. So I think the conversation stuff's really important in the overall process". Jessica's thinking was similar: "If I've already journaled and got a bit clearer and then can be a bit more specific about what's gnawing, then to have the conversation is a lot more useful because there's more chance that what it is that's gnawing will then be addressed and I'll get a way forward".

Framework 2:	Proactive Resistance, Rehearsal, Agency and Action
Narrative 4:	Transformative choices, opportunities and accomplishments
Thread 19:	Reflection and change

Reflecting on plans, commitments and accomplishments provides women with confirmation and affirmation of the choices they have made, or plan to make; their

stronger and more defined sense of self, identity and self-value; a greater awareness of their emotions and how these link to their thoughts, actions and perceptions; and a stronger declaration of their own needs, priorities and rights. Naomi
journaled strongly, "I've been doing the passive 'I deserve it' thing, but now I
need to be doing the active expectation thing. "I have to put myself out there—I'm
going to try the doors in front of me. F***—now I'm scared!" Jessica journaled
"(I have) ended a cycle, completed a journey. I have gained a better sense of
proportion, balance—not all work and no play, fun and silliness, greater comfort
with myself".

Conclusion

Journaling is a form of action characterised by consciousness-raising and resistance
(see Chap. 6). The notion of journaling as active resistance to dominant stereotypes
and social and gender expectations of women, removes the idea of journaling as a
process of solitary passiveness and ineffective rumination. There are many
components to the frameworks, narratives and threads that make up the Women's
Journaling Group Program model. The program—and the model—can initially
seem overwhelming and complicated because of this. I hope that the women's
journaling extracts provided some clarity around what the different component
parts look like and how the model can be used to develop journaling activities and
programs for journaling groups. The next chapter is brief and provides an example
outline of A Women's Journaling Group and possible activities and processes.

Chapter 9
An Example Outline of a Women's Journaling Group Program

Abstract What follows is a brief agenda and outline of the processes and activities within one example of a Women's Journaling Group Program. This program could be facilitated over a period of a few weeks or concertinaed into one or two whole days. The narratives and threads that could be addressed in each activity are noted.

Keywords Journaling · Feminist group work · Depression

Women's Journaling Group

Date:

General Introduction and Welcome (I will have already met each woman in an initial individual interview prior to the commencement of the group)

Introduction to the Group

Name: Women's Journaling Group (WJG)

Aims:

- To give women information about Journaling
- To provide women with opportunities to try out different Journaling activities and techniques
- To explore how Journaling might assist women to understand their depression and themselves
- To explore how Journaling might uncover and reveal links between women's experiences of violence and their depression
- To imagine different futures and how change might occur

D. Western, *Gender-based Violence and Depression in Women*,
SpringerBriefs in Social Work, DOI: 10.1007/978-1-4614-7532-3_9,

Structure and Processes within the Group:

I will provide some overall information about Journaling to begin (include my own experiences) and the rest of the session will provide time for women to try out different journal activities and techniques

- Open to sharing and learning from each other. Share only what women want to share.
- Importance of safety and respect within the group.
- Record the themes and ideas that come from the women's Journaling through the day on sheets of paper on the walls. Important to be able to see their thoughts, ideas and words as well as to hear them. Makes them real and gives them strength.
- The Women's Journaling Group follows the process in the model—moving from reflection, acknowledgment and contemplation through to action, change, resistance and agency.
- Complete evaluations of each session throughout the day to give women an opportunity to reflect on their learning, thoughts and feelings and integrate this reflection with the next session of Journaling and discussion. This also gives me feedback about women's experiences and how the group is going for them.
- Women's Journaling is not collected but the women's evaluations are. Provide copies for women if they would like a record of their evaluations.

Getting to Know You Time:

Introduction to each other: Activity—Photolanguage cards. Choose a card that describes you/your situation. Share in pairs, then in the whole group. Pull out ideas/themes and record on paper.

Group Guidelines:

Brainstorm. What will help to make the group feel safe and comfortable for you? Start discussion in pairs, then share with the whole group.

What is Journaling?

Information and women's thoughts. (was discussed in the pre-group interview, but a good starting place for the group.) Record ideas and display around the room.

Journaling 1

Feedback, sharing, discussion, reflection, evaluation, looking at ideas/themes emerging will occur between activities and throughout the day.

Journal activity 1: Sentence starters. 'When thinking about the sort of person I am, I would describe myself as ....' (The Narratives and Threads that are covered: identity, sense of self and self-value; the emergence of women's voices; reconnection with the self and re-establishment of identity).

Journal activity 2: Sentence starters. 'I think people expect me to … and then I feel …' (Narratives/Threads: structural and social roles, relationships and expectations; conflicts between these and women's sense of self, identity and own needs; identification and expression of emotion; the emergence of women's voices: the expression of emotion; reconnection with the self and re-establishment of identity: conflict between inner and outer worlds; new insights).

Journal activity 3: Lists. List the relationships that nurture and strengthen you and, in a separate list, the relationships that bring you stress, frustration or sadness. Choose one and journal about how this relationship influences your depression. (Narratives/Threads: structural and social roles, relationships and expectations; identification and expression of emotion; assessing and re-assessing connections with other people; new insights: understandings, connections and transformations: resistance, change and transformation).

Journal activity 4. Lists. List the things that give you meaning and purpose in your life. Choose one and journal about how it influences your depression. (Narratives/Threads: identity, sense of self and self-value; Transformative choices, opportunities and accomplishments; the emergence of women's voices; new insights, understandings, connections and transformations; Rehearsal: opportunities for planning, considering alternatives, making choices; Identification and expression of enlivening feelings and affirmative experiences; resistance and transformative action).

Evaluation of Session 1

- What has it been like to journal about the narratives and threads we've discussed this morning?
- How relevant have these issues been to your experience of depression?

Journaling 2

Journaling activity 5: Clusters. Cluster around the idea of choice. (I'll show an example of a cluster I have done). Explore the words and themes that have emerged in the cluster. Journal about one of the major themes and what this means for your understanding of your depression. (Narratives/Threads: identity, sense of self and self-value; transformative choices, opportunities and accomplishments; the emergence of women's voices; consciousness-raising; new insights, understandings, connections and transformations; rehearsal: opportunities for planning, considering alternatives, making choices; resistance, change and transformation; imagination, creativity and consideration of a hopeful future).

Journaling activity 6: Sentence starter: "When I feel invisible and insignificant, I ….". (Narratives/Threads: identification and expression of emotion;

structural and social roles, relationships and expectations; expression and change; the emergence of women's voices; new insights, understandings, connections and transformations).

Journaling activity 7: Sentence starter: "It is important to me for my voice and my needs to be heard because ... and then my depression ...." (Narratives/ Threads: identity, sense of self and self-value; transformative choices, opportunities and accomplishments; the emergence of women's voices; consciousness-raising; new insights, understandings, connections and transformations; the transformed and stronger sense of identity, self and self-value; resistance and transformative action).

Journaling activity 8: Sentence starter: "I think I would be most likely to journal when I am depressed or angry or both because ....." (Narratives/Threads: identification and expression of emotion; transformative choices, opportunities and accomplishments; the emergence of women's voices; expression and change: depression and anger as motivators; crucial movement and a sense of change; new insights, understandings, connections and transformations; resistance and transformative action).

Evaluation of Session 2

- I am finding that, for me, Journaling .....
- I think that sharing in the group ......

Journaling 3

Journaling activity 9: Inside Out Journaling Kit. Choose an activity and a topic from the cards in the kit and complete. Women may also decide to use a Journaling technique that we haven't looked at yet: for example, dialogue.

Journaling activity 10: Collage. Using the idea of **proactive resistance and action**, think about how action occurs in women's journals and use these ideas as prompts for women to respond to in their collage. Potential questions for the Journaling collage have been developed from these ideas. Each question will be asked in relation to how it relates to the women understanding and managing their depression and the associated concerns. Not all questions need be asked. The questions are:

- How do you ask for guidance and support?
- What are the affirmative aspects of life on which you can focus?
- What questions about hope and the future do you ask?
- How do you use anger, resistance and strength?

- What are your needs and priorities and how do you make them known?
- How do you change the stories you and/or others hold about you?
- What are the choices that are important for you to identify and make?
- What is your secure and genuine sense of yourself and your identity?
- What are some new ways of thinking you would like to try? How might you act on this awareness, and do something different from the current or past situation?

Journal about your collage to find some extra insights.

Many of the narratives and threads are covered in this activity which makes it an excellent activity to use in the last session of a group. Various opportunities exist for consciousness-raising, resistance, transformation, imagination, creativity and creation of a hopeful future, reflection and change to take place.

Final Evaluation of all sessions and the Group

In this evaluation, women can also check the written records of the themes that have emerged during the Group and list the ones that are relevant and meaningful to them. Women's evaluation can come from their learnings; the changes they might have made in their understandings and perspectives; the challenges they still face; their level and nature of feelings and emotions; and their experience of participating in the Group.

- What I have learned about depression and me from being part of the Women's Journaling Group ....
- What has changed for me is .....
- If other women with depression asked me if Journaling was helpful, I would say .....
- I might include Journaling in my life now by .....
- My experience of participating in the Women's Journaling Group was ....
- If I made changes to the Women's Journaling Group, I would ....

The final group activity includes a summary of learning that has occurred, group processes and dynamics, changes in women's thinking and behaviour, future ideas and plans. Where to from here?

Goodbye activity

Some example questions from a post-group follow up evaluation

Statement 1: I have continued to journal even though the Women's Journaling Group has finished.

1 2 3 4 5

Comment:_____

Statement 2: I do not have happy memories of the Women's Journaling Group.

1 2 3 4 5

Comment:_____

Statement 3: Journaling has provided me with some insights and understandings about my depression.

1 2 3 4 5

Comment:_____

Statement 4: Sharing our Journaling in the group helped me to gain further understandings about my depression.

1 2 3 4 5

Comment:_____

Statement 5: I journal in a different way when I'm on my own than the way I journalled when I was in the group.

1 2 3 4 5

Comment:_____

Statement 6: I would make changes to the Women's Journaling Group.

1 2 3 4 5

Please comment: _____

Final question: What has been the most important insight or piece of learning you have taken from the Women's Journaling Group?

Chapter 10
Practice Guidelines for Facilitating a Women's Journaling Group Programme

Abstract This chapter provides practice guidelines for practitioners who are interested in undertaking journaling work with women and facilitating women's journaling groups. The guidelines cover practice theory and knowledge as well as content and process issues that may arise when facilitating women's journaling groups for women who have experienced gender-based violence and depression. The guidelines are informed by and based on the Women's Journaling Group Programme model. As a result, the practice guidelines reflect and summarise themes and topics that have been discussed in the preceding chapters of this book. This material includes the experiences of depression and gender-based violence for women; the critical-feminist-intersectional theoretical understanding of depression and gender-based violence that underpins social work practice with women in the model; the role that journaling may play in women's lives and recovery; the theory underpinning feminist group work; the frameworks, narratives and threads within the model and the methods and principles of consciousness-raising and resistance. Presenting the guidelines in this chapter—and at the conclusion of the book— brings this text towards a close. I hope the practice guidelines provide practical thoughts and ideas to enable practitioners to develop their own women's journaling groups based on the model outlined in this book.

Keywords Women's Journaling Group Programme · Journaling · Depression · Practice guidelines · Gender-based violence · Consciousness-raising · Feminist

Practice Guideline One: Broad Understandings of Journaling are Needed

Broad definitions of journaling are crucial for social workers to hold. Social workers can then clearly explain to women the range of activities that may constitute journaling and the different ways in which journaling can be undertaken. What is key is that women find their own way to journal.

D. Western, *Gender-based Violence and Depression in Women*,
SpringerBriefs in Social Work, DOI: 10.1007/978-1-4614-7532-3_10,
© The Author(s) 2013

Women feel more confident to engage in journaling when they are presented with a range of activities, including those where writing is not the focus. This allows the activity of journaling to be available to more women experiencing depression, including women like Phoebe, who whilst not comfortable with writing as a method to express herself, was still able to develop narratives and themes that told her story using non-traditional journaling techniques. The ability to express oneself and find one's voice as a way of re-establishing and reconnecting with one's identity, and therefore managing and recovering from depression, is central for women.

Practice Guideline Two: The Range of Journaling Activities Should be Varied

Linked to Practice Guideline One is the importance of social workers encouraging women to experiment with journaling. This experimentation assists women to experience being more closely connected to their creative skills and capacity; important in being able to comprehensively and genuinely express themselves, clarify their sense of self and have choice and control over the way they do this. Social workers need to be flexible in the ways they provide journaling activities to women. There need to be inbuilt opportunities for women to try different activities, techniques and materials in order to find their own style of journaling. Time to reflect on the frequency of journaling that might suit each woman, the length of time journaling might be kept and the manner in which journaling can be incorporated safely into women's everyday lives must be provided in journaling groups.

Practice Guideline Three: Re-reading and Reflecting on Journaling Content can be Helpful for Women

Re-reading earlier journaling entries can assist women to reach deeper understandings of their feelings, thoughts and experiences, to find patterns in them, make links between them and integrate insights and understandings into stronger senses of self. The reflection and evaluation activities in the journaling groups provide opportunities for some re-reading and review to occur. Re-reading and reflecting upon the content of their journals can be a therapeutic, and potentially preventative, strategy for women. The emotional safety of women with depression during therapy, counselling and support is a key area of attention for social workers. Bearing in mind that journaling can raise unexpected and emotionally challenging thoughts and memories, social workers need to prepare women for re-reading their journal entries. Re-reading may occur in privacy in the group, prior to the group as part of individual counselling that is held alongside Women's

Journaling Group programmes, and/or any other location in which women feel safe. Reflection and debriefing need to be offered to women following their re-reading of journals.

Practice Guideline Four: Women's Experience and Expression of Anger is Beneficial

In any therapeutic response such as women's journaling groups, activities underpinned by feminist understandings of anger in women will provide a space for women to explore the meaning of their anger. Anger may take some time to emerge fully and women need to be supported through the processes of identifying, expressing and experiencing anger. Experimenting with ways to express anger and to do so in safe ways that do not overwhelm their capacity to use anger constructively can be revelatory for women. A level of safety may take some time to attain, and therefore women's confidence in naming and expressing their anger in a journaling group may take some time too. Social workers need to be familiar with the ways in which anger may be expressed by women and be comfortable for working with women expressing uncertainty, fear and reluctance to explore emotions that are alarming to them. Social workers also need to be skilled in holding, monitoring, containing and responding to high levels of emotion, and the impacts such emotion may have on group dynamics. Knowledge of the long-term nature of some memories, thoughts and feelings for women and the impact that memories may have on women's mental health and confidence is essential. This knowledge is linked with knowledge about trauma-related therapeutic work.

Practice Guideline Five: Women's Anger, Change and Decision Making Capacity may be Connected

When women reach a point of wishing to make changes in their life and decisions to achieve these changes, a new level of uncertainty may arise regarding their self-confidence and capacity. Decision making can be an extremely demanding activity and some women may question their ability to gauge what constitutes sound decision making. Journaling activities to explore the concept of decision making can be useful and group discussion can assist with resolving questions and uncertainty. Social workers need understandings about theories of change and decision making. Given that anger can be a motivator for change, practitioners would benefit from having a sound understanding of the dynamics and meanings of anger in women who have experienced violence and depression. Anger is also discussed in Practice Guideline Four.

Practice Guideline Six: A Future Focus is Important for Women's Recovery

Without minimising the importance of the experiences and emotions associated with depression, social workers need to ensure that, at some stage, journaling also has a focus on hope, the discovery of joy and the possibility of a positive future. Journaling activities can be introduced to women within the Proactive Resistance, Rehearsal, Agency and Action Framework when women are ready and secure in themselves to have the capacity to look ahead and begin some planning around how their future might look different from their past. The collage activity in the Women's Journaling Group example in Chap. 9 is an example of an activity that encourages women's creativity and openness to journal about their possible futures.

Practice Guideline Seven: Reclamation of a Sense of Self is an Ongoing Process

Whilst women do achieve a stronger, positive sense of self over time, their sense of self can remain quite vulnerable to undermining from other people and subsequent episodes of low mood and depression. This will be especially true if women continue experiencing violence. Consequently, therapeutic work with women in relation to their sense of self and self-value would most usefully occur over an extended period. Women's journaling is a recursive process which moves back and forward between the two frameworks, the four narratives and the different threads. Social workers can use this recursive process in the way they work with women in relation to their sense of self over time; this can be a process of revisiting and rebuilding from previously attained awareness, insight, resistance, action and growth. Social workers need to be skilled in working alongside women to normalise this back and forth process and reassure women that this constitutes their own particular pattern of recovery.

Practice Guideline Eight: The Role of 'Hope' in Recovery and in Women's Journaling Groups is Influential

Houghton (2007) notes that hope is a complex and multi-faceted concept. Integrating the notion of hope in relation to recovery, wellness or indeed to journaling group processes and dynamics, into journaling group content is crucial. The sense of hopefulness and possibility ebbs and flows during the lifetime of a group as do the dynamics between group members. Women have great influence on each others' confidence and belief in hope. Social workers need to be attuned to changing dynamics within the group, language that suggests changes in the level of hope, confidence and agency and to reflect on these processes with group members. Group facilitators may need to take the role of 'hope holder' when group members are not able to do this through lack of confidence, doubts or experiences which have damaged their sense of hope. Social workers need to clarify their own understandings of 'hope' in order to be open to other perceptions. Similarly, social workers need to listen to women's understandings of hope and explore, with women, how these understandings can contribute to their recovery from depression. Less-structured journaling activities such as collage or clustering may be useful in encouraging women to freely explore their understandings of hope and what it might enable. However, other women may prefer more containing activities such as list making in order to narrow the potentially overwhelming number of possibilities.

Practice Guideline Nine: Resistance is a Method and Activity for Change

The modelling of resistance in the journal and through discussions with other women in journaling groups can encourage women to think in different ways about their depression. This constitutes another way in which micro-political forms of resistance can contribute to change on a level broader than the individual. Social workers need to be flexible in their definitions and understandings of what constitutes 'resistance' and to be capable of introducing and facilitating discussions about different modes and meanings of resistance within women's journaling groups. Social workers also need to be clear about their own values and beliefs in relation to activities such as consciousness raising and resistance and how these activities might translate into practice. Reflection about practicing from feminist, critical and intersectional perspectives will strengthen social work practice.

Practice Guideline Ten: Depression is a Shared Yet Unique Experience for Women

A feminist knowledge of working with women experiencing depression and a solid understanding of the structural and systemic issues that contribute to the development and continuation of depression in women is vital. When women know that experiences of depression—and violence—can be similar and shared, yet understood and responded to it in different ways, the acceptance of their individual identities and senses of self can be strengthened. Social workers need to have an awareness and understanding of the different lenses through which women may understand their experiences of depression. Aligned with this awareness is the willingness and competence to reflect upon one's own assumptions and interpretations about women and depression and about the ways in which women might resist the factors contributing to the development of their depression. Having an understanding of what it might mean, to social workers and to women, when women do not appear to be 'resisting' is also important for non-judgemental practice. Building regular time into women's journaling groups for women to share and reflect on the different ways they think about their depression will assist them to gain insight into their own understandings, perspectives and strategies as well as into those of other women.

Practice Guideline Eleven: Activities to Assist Women to Operationalise Their Decisions for Change are Essential

Whilst women may resist societal demands and expectations in their journals and in journaling activities and discussions in women's journaling groups, the challenge comes when they are faced with putting their desired changes into action outside the group. Within women's journaling groups, practitioners need to work with women to assist them to implement their chosen changes and plans in their day-to-day lives. Reflection and evaluation activities can provide opportunities for women to check and monitor their progress and receive support and ideas from other group members. Social workers need to be inventive and creative in their work with women to assist them to operationalise changes they wish to make. Discussion with women about how they might journal once the journaling group has concluded can be helpful too. A follow-up journaling session or group can provide encouragement for women to continue journaling, if this is what they wish to do, and provide an opportunity for women to share changes that have been made in their lives. Women may benefit from guidance about what themes, for example they could explore or look for in their journaling. Tips and suggestions for journaling outside the group, as well as journaling ideas and tasks to take away can be encouraging.

Practice Guideline Twelve: Practitioners Need to Have Solid Knowledge About Working with Critical Feminist and Intersectional Theories and Concepts

Authors such as Dominelli (2002a, b), Fook (1993, 2002) and Mullaly (2007) provide ideas and frameworks which inform and guide feminist and critical social work practice. Other useful references are included in the reference list in Chap. 3. Careful consideration and planning are required when working with women to resist societal expectations and the 'good woman' role; social workers need to ensure that women do not develop feelings of guilt or responsibility for taking on those roles in the first instance. Therefore, practitioners need to be able to provide a strong feminist understanding for women about factors that contribute to gender-based violence and the development of depression in women. In addition, social workers need to be skilled at finding a balance in their facilitation between guiding group members and activities to ensure group purposes, aims, development and process are achieved on the one hand, and enabling members to exercise self-determination, choice, participation and development of safety and connections with other members on the other. A balance is also needed between the focus on the content and outcome of journaling activities and the process involved in undertaking the activity. What was learned, for example, during reflection on the themes that a particular journaling activity uncovered for women?

Practice Guideline Thirteen: Journaling can be Employed in a Preventative Manner

Using journaling in a preventative manner potentially broadens the scope of journaling as a therapeutic tool. This Guideline links very closely with Practice Guideline Three which discusses the role that re-reading of journals may have as a therapeutic strategy. Some material in journals can be distressing to remember; on the other hand, that same material can encourage women when they realise what they have accomplished and the impact of these changes on their mental health and their life styles. Social workers can take an active role with women in their use of preventative journaling by highlighting options for the different methods, styles, types of content and direction in which women can use journals. Journaling activities, group discussions and reflections that focus on women's achievements, strengths and the changes they make contribute to preventative work.

Practice Guideline Fourteen: Privacy and Confidentiality is Crucial in Women's Journaling Groups

Social workers need to respect the privacy of women's journals and the confidentiality women require in order to be able to journal honestly, and therefore most effectively. Reminding women in a journaling group to respect the privacy and confidentiality of each other and their journaling is a crucial guideline for group participants. Sharing one's journaling is not common. Thus, sharing one's thoughts, feelings and concerns with other women in a journaling group can be difficult, but it is a vital part of the women's journaling group programme. Expanding on the meanings of their journaling within the group is valuable for women because it adds to the understandings they begin in their journaling. In the early stages of a journaling group when invited to share, women may feel embarrassed, ashamed or 'the odd one out'. Social workers and women need to negotiate the safest way for information in the journal to be shared. To begin with, women may simply share the outcome of their journaling or talk about what they journalled rather than read out the journaling. The opportunity for women to verbalise and express their efforts to understand their depression and its impact on their lives, enables them to have their experiences and efforts witnessed and validated by other women in the group. For a high level of support and validation to exist in a therapeutic group, there needs to be a high degree of trust, understanding and benevolence amongst group members. The group facilitator has a role in developing, nurturing, sustaining and encouraging group members, not only as a group, but as independent individuals (McDermott 2002). Having a therapist 'correct' one's thoughts and ideas in one's journal disregards feminist practice and the notion of the woman making her own decisions about her own life. See also Practice Guideline seventeen.

Practice Guideline Fifteen: Preparatory and Beginning Phases of Women's Journaling Groups Provide Structure for Women

A comprehensive overview of journaling provides a welcoming and informative introduction for women participating in women's journaling groups. This introduction could cover areas such as a brief history of women and journaling; different definitions and types of journaling; and some ideas about how women have used journals on their own and/or in therapeutic ways. An individual preliminary meeting with each woman prior to the commencement of the journaling group provides an opportunity for the worker and each woman to get to know each other a little before meeting in the group. This can contribute to the development of a sense of safety, trust and familiarity for women as they go into the first group session. This preliminary meeting also acts as part of a worker's assessment about a woman's readiness to participate in a journaling group. A sense of each woman's history, depression and violence experiences and ways of relating can be obtained so workers have some background information prior to the commencement of the group. Finally, a preliminary meeting can provide an opportunity for workers to give an initial explanation of what journaling involves and give women a couple of journaling activities to try prior to the group so they gain a sense of what journaling might be like for them.

Practice Guideline Sixteen: Assessment of Women's Readiness to Participate in a Journaling Group is Necessary

A holistic feminist assessment of women and their situations is crucial in order to ensure that women are ready, safe and comfortable to participate in a group with other women. Fook (2002, p. 125) writing from a critical perspective suggests that the concept of 'constructing professional narratives' replaces that of 'making professional assessments' as a way of learning about clients' multiple and changing contexts and needs, and doing so beyond the existing power relations, structures and discourses. Simonds (2001) presents a modified version of the 'Aspects of the Self Model' to enable social workers to understand and learn about the experiences of depressed women through their conversations about their frames of reference, self-capacities and core cognitive schemas. The presence or otherwise of suicidal ideation and/or intent is another factor to consider. McDermott (2002) provides a thorough overview of the factors that social workers might consider when recruiting or inviting women to join groups. Herman (1992) suggests that women are most likely to benefit from participating in a therapeutic group when they are safe from traumatic situations, able to maintain their self-care, have stabilised any symptoms of their illness, have reliable support outside the group, can commit to regular group attendance and manage the issues that are likely to be raised by other women in the group. Not all women will be comfortable working in a group and prefer to seek support individually from friends, family or practitioners.

Practice Guideline Seventeen: Building Trust Between Group Members is Critical

This guideline builds on Practice Guideline Fourteen. Building trust between women is crucial particularly where sensitive issues such as depression and violence are the focus of discussion. Social workers need to give attention to the types of activities that will enable group members to engage with each other and with the therapeutic purpose of the group. Ideally, the development of trust amongst all members within a group grows stronger as the group continues, whether the group runs for a single session or over the longer term. However, the development of trust needs to be an immediate focus within the development of a group and goes hand in hand with the changing dynamics and different stages of group development. The early to middle stages within women's groups are the pre-affiliation; establishing a relational base; mutuality and interpersonal empathy stages (Schiller 1997). This is where facilitators can encourage and facilitate group activities that promote and assist the development of trust. Introductory exercises, discussions about different topics and shared experiences in pairs and then in the whole group are helpful ways of doing this. The facilitator's modelling of sharing her own experiences in group discussions can also provide some guidance and reassurance for women of how to interact and share their own experiences.

Practice Guideline Eighteen: Women's Groups Proceed Through Developmental Stages that are Specific to Each Women's Group

The relational model (Schiller 1997) and feminist understandings of group development and process have implications for women's journaling group facilitators. The stages of group development in women's groups described by Schiller (1997, see Chap. 6) are useful to consider. Change and development for women might occur through gentle and respectful challenge and confrontation from other group members in an atmosphere of mutuality and interpersonal empathy. Time given to reflection within the group throughout the day is a valuable way for women to learn about the changes that are possible for them, the ways in which they might engage in change and to identify the beginnings of changes that are already emerging.

Practice Guideline Nineteen: Women's Journaling Groups can be Conducted Over a Day or During a Number of Weeks

Some women prefer attending a women's journaling group over a short, contained period of time like a day, whereas other women choose to attend the group over a period of weeks. The Women's Journaling Group Programme model allows for flexibility in the period of time in which groups are facilitated. The length and time lines of women's journaling groups might also make a difference to the level of support that women request at the completion of the group. Advantages of facilitating a group over a day are that women get to know each other quickly and a sense of safety, trust and familiarity can be developed within the group in a short period of time. The rhythm of journaling, feedback, discussion, reflection and learning is also established and reinforced throughout the day which adds to the sense of predictability and belonging. Themes in women's journaling emerge through the day and consistencies in these themes throughout the day can be identified quite easily by the facilitator and by the women themselves. Disadvantages of a one day session compared with group sessions over a number of weeks can be that relationships and understandings do not have the opportunity to richly develop over time. Women's familiarity and confidence with the notion of journaling may not develop if one day is insufficient to answer their questions about how they might journal and how journaling might assist them in their understanding and management of depression. Time for reflection on the journaling process and themes that arise during a women's journaling group held over a number of weeks may enable women to engage in the process more slowly, learn from each other and more easily integrate journaling into their lives. Therapeutic outcomes are more likely to be long lived and useful when journaling is undertaken on a regular basis over several sessions rather than on one or two brief occasions. The decision depends on myriad factors including women's preferences, facilitators' availability, venue availability, funding and resources and organisational policy and procedure.

Practice Guideline Twenty: Undertake Evaluations of Women's Journaling Groups

Evaluations of the content and the process provide information for practitioners about the effectiveness and relevance of the programme. Feedback from women about the usefulness of particular journaling activities, what they learned and what helped them learn and make changes is valuable information for practitioners to have as they further develop and refine journaling groups. Ongoing mini evaluations during each session enable women to provide feedback to practitioners about the programme but also to reflect on their own experience of the group, the activities and their own development as the sessions progress. Examples of mini evaluation questions embedded in the journaling group programme and a post-group evaluation are found in Chap. 9.

References

Dominelli L (2002a) Anti-oppressive social work theory and practice. Palgrave Macmillan, Basingstoke

Dominelli L (2002b) Feminist social work theory and practice. Palgrave, Basingstoke

Fook J (1993) Radical casework: a theory of practice. Allen and Unwin, St Leonards

Fook J (2002) Social work: critical theory and practice. Sage, London

Herman J (1992) Trauma and Recovery: from domestic abuse to political terror. London: Basic Books

Houghton S (2007) Exploring hope: its meaning for adults living with depression and for social work practice. Journal 6(3)

McDermott F (2002) Inside group work: a guide to reflective practice. Allen and Unwin, Crows Nest

Mullaly B (2007) The new structural social work. Oxford University Press, Don Mills

Schiller L (1997) Rethinking stages of development in women's groups: Implications for practice. Social Work with Groups 20(3):3–19

Simonds S (2001) Depression and women: an integrative treatment approach. Springer Publishing Company Inc., New York

Chapter 11
Postscript

Uncertainties remain about the most efficacious manner in which to support, respond to and manage depression in women. As practitioners, we work with many, many women and we need to have a broad array of activities and resources to offer them as they work to regain and/or redevelop their safety, confidence, sense of self and trust in the world around them. Above all, my hope is that this book will be of interest to a wide range of readers and, as a result, that women who have experienced violence and depression will be offered, and will find that, journaling with the support, encouragement and validation from other women can provide new possibilities for living well.

D. Western, *Gender-based Violence and Depression in Women*,
SpringerBriefs in Social Work, DOI: 10.1007/978-1-4614-7532-3_11,
© The Author(s) 2013

Index

D. Western, *Gender-based Violence and Depression in Women*,
SpringerBriefs in Social Work, DOI: 10.1007/978-1-4614-7532-3,
© The Author(s) 2013